5

Out *of* step

jane murray heimlich

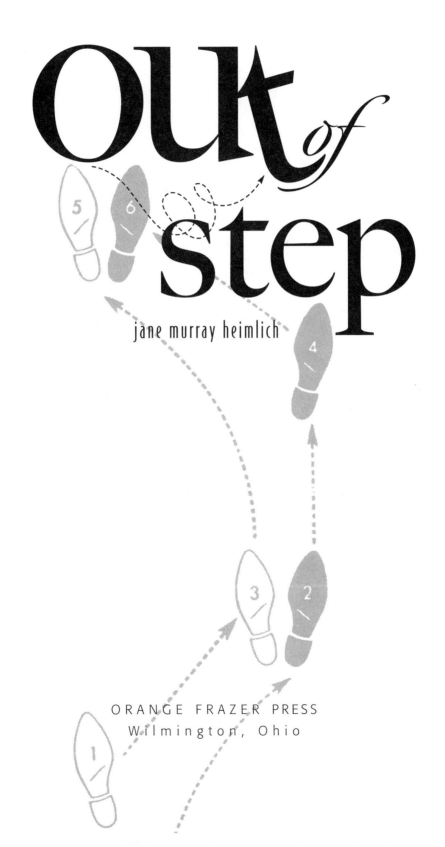

ORANGE FRAZER PRESS
Wilmington, Ohio

ISBN 978-1933197-661

Additional copies of *Out of Step* may be ordered directly from:
Orange Frazer Press
P.O. Box 214
Wilmington, OH 45177

Telephone 1.800.852.9332 for price and shipping information.
Website: *www.orangefrazer.com*

Design: Jeff Fulwiler

Library of Congress Cataloging-in-Publication Data

Heimlich, Jane.
  Out of step / by Jane Murray Heimlich.
     p. cm.
  ISBN 978-1-933197-66-1
  1. Heimlich, Jane. 2. Dancers--United States--Biography. 3.
Wives--United States--Biography. I. Title.
  GV1785.H455 2009
  792.802'8092--dc22
                                          2009013857

To friend and writer, Mari Messer, who never lost faith in this memoir

Table of contents

INTRODUCTION / *page xiii*

Part I—MEET THE FAMILY

Chapter one / FAMILY SECRETS / *page four*

Chapter two / THE DANCING MISSIONARY / *page fourteen*

Chapter three / MOVING TO HOLLYWOOD / *page twenty-two*

Chapter four / FAMILY SECRETS / *page thirty-four*

Chapter five / LIFE IN THE SPOTLIGHT / *page forty-six*

Part II—THE YOUNG JANE MURRAY

Chapter six / NEW YORK BACHELOR DAYS / *page fifty-four*

Chapter seven / THE HAPPY HOUSEWIFE / *page sixty-four*

Chapter eight / LAUNCHING MYSELF / *page seventy-four*

Chapter nine / BEFORE THE MANEUVER / *page eighty-two*

Chapter ten / CELEBRITY HOOPLA / *page eighty-eight*

Part III—IN SEARCH OF MY FATHER

Chapter eleven / AN IMMIGRANT'S JOURNEY / *page ninety-six*

Chapter twelve / A YIDDISH MACHIAVELLI / *page one hundred four*

Chapter thirteen / MOISHE BECOMES ARTHUR MURRAY / *page one hundred ten*

Chapter fourteen / WHEN ARTHUR MEETS KATHRYN / *page one hundred eighteen*

Chapter fifteen / KATHRYN SWINGS FROM A CHANDELIER / *page one hundred twenty-six*

Part IV—TAKING A SECOND LOOK

Chapter sixteen / A DAUGHTER'S LAMENT / *page one hundred thirty-six*

Chapter seventeen / MY REAL MOTHER / *page one hundred forty-two*

Chapter eighteen / MIDLIFE CRISIS / *page one hundred fifty-two*

Chapter nineteen / RESISTANCE FROM THE OLD GUARD / *page one hundred sixty-two*

Chapter twenty / COMING FULL CIRCLE / *page one hundred seventy*

Chapter twenty-one / THE LAST DANCE / *page one hundred eighty-two*

Acknowledgments

My heartfelt thanks to:

My assistant, Teresa (Terri) Malloy who is simply the smartest most capable person I know.

Georgia Court, Lawson Wulsin, Janet Metzelaar, and other members of our Writers Group who listened enthusiastically to each chapter and offered insightful commentary.

My editor, John Baskin of Orange Frazer Press, who kept his sense of humor while he double-checked the details and guided the final edit.

Marcy Hawley, publisher of Orange Frazer Press, who is the reason I'm here.

Gordon Baer, gifted photographer and long-time friend, who has marked the publication of each of my books with a portrait.

My husband, Hank, who always knows when I need encouragement.

My children for their individual talents. Early in the game, Elisabeth had the sense to spot the good family photos and squirrel them away. Janet, fellow writer, listened to the woes of her mother and offered good advice.

My parents, who taught me by example the importance of hard work and determination.

My Uncle Ira, a vigorous 104, who has been an invaluable family historian.

Introduction

Several years ago, I arrived late at a party in Chattanooga, Tennessee, where my husband, Dr. Henry Heimlich, was being honored for devising the Heimlich Maneuver. The party was already in full swing. My hostess took me by the hand, led me into the living room, and proclaimed with a charming Southern accent, "And here is *Mrs. Maneuver!*"

That's the story of my life, I thought wryly as I chatted with guests who voiced honey-dipped words of welcome. I realized once again the effect of being related to fame. I've had considerable experience. As Mrs. Maneuver, I listened to countless stories about how a rescuer saved a choking victim with "the Heimlich." I was truly impressed by the way so many people, even small children, spring into action to save a life using the Maneuver. But once in a while, I hungered for someone to turn to me and say, "What are you doing these days?"

In my own family, as the daughter of Arthur Murray, I also felt out of step with my well-known parents. My father founded the dancing schools that bear his name, and, in 1950, became a television personality when he and my mother, Kathryn, starred on *The Arthur Murray Party*. Growing up, I felt certain that a famous dancer's daughter was expected to be lively and outgoing. So I spent many years trying to be Miss Sparkle Plenty rather than my own quiet self.

My mother emceed *The Arthur Murray Party* and emerged as a star in her own right. Like many who tuned in, I admired my parents and felt a tug of emotion watching them waltz off at the end of the show. I marveled at my mother's daredevil exploits, some as bizarre as hanging from a chandelier. Even more astonishing was the way she held her own in comedy skits with seasoned performers like Bert Lahr and Groucho Marx.

But the day-to-day life of being a daughter of two TV stars evoked quite different feelings. My twin sister, Phyllis, and I, found it nearly impossible to live up to our parents' ideals of perfection. Frankly, we were afraid of our father. His biting criticism lashed out when least expected. Mother was described by *TV Guide* and other magazines as a wonder woman, up at daybreak baking my father's favorite honey cake. By 9 o'clock she was at her office at the dancing studio where she corresponded with branch managers and wrote sales and training manuals for pupils and teachers.

My mother's constant busyness discouraged me from sharing my concerns about not fitting in. If I ventured to tell her about a boy I had just met, undoubtedly the phone would ring. "*Time* magazine has some questions about a TV feature." "*Family Circle* needs more photos." "*Ladies Home Journal* wants an interview." What chance did I have to compete for her attention?

The situation was no better with my father. If I found myself trapped in a conversation with him, I staved off his criticism by complimenting him on a recent article or a wisecrack that appeared in Walter Winchell's column.

I longed for a house in which people talked nonsense, giggled, and had fun. There was little nonsense in our house. There was always something to be achieved. We talked only at meals, the conversation as ordered as a menu. A subtle tension overhung the New York apartment: Father's abiding criticisms, Mother's needs to have him admire her, Phyllis and I suspended somewhere between.

Some years after both my parents had died in their 90s, I got tired of dragging around heavy loads of resentment. It occurred to me that in order to deal with these feelings I needed to know what made my parents the way they were. I knew very little about my father's background, except that he was raised on New York's Lower East Side, a teeming slum, prodded by his formidable mother, Sara. I set out on a journey of discovery.

Anyone who has made it the hard way in America, or has a family member who experienced such a struggle, will relate to my father's rags-to-riches saga. His dancing skills and business acumen served as a passport to a life of wealth and acclaim. A dancing teacher at 19 at an exclusive resort in Asheville, North Carolina, he hobnobbed with Southern socialites. In the early 1920s, the Arthur Murray school of dancing that he founded in New York flourished under his direction. His uncanny knowledge of what the public wanted led to his launching the television show *The Arthur Murray Party*, which featured leading stars of the entertainment world.

Those who observed my parents together, whether on television or at a social gathering, thought that Kathryn ran the show. Her quick wit bouncing off Arthur's hesitant speech made her balding, poker-faced husband look positively foolish. In reality, it was all an act on his part. He was the real boss.

In many ways, Kathryn was more like daddy's little girl than his wife. When Arthur criticized her—which he often did—she was plunged into depression. No one knows for certain, but I suspect it was depression that ultimately led to her near-fatal suicide attempt.

By the time I graduated from boarding school and finished college, I was eager to be on my own. Fortunately, a college friend asked me to share her apartment off Fifth Avenue in New York. It didn't matter that my first abode was one room in a basement. Later, as a wife and mother living in a ranch house in a New York suburb, I tried to be the typical 1950s happy homemaker. Feeling like Betty Furness, who pranced around a gleaming refrigerator in General Electric commercials, I vacuumed my living room in a skirt and high-heeled pumps.

In the '50s and '60s, it was difficult enough for a woman to be seen as a person, then fate handed me a double whammy. My husband, a little known but highly respected chest surgeon, made a name for himself and suddenly became a household word. *Here we go again*, I thought. I was catapulted back into a world I thought I had left behind, a world in which I played second fiddle to fame.

Despite having TV-star parents and a husband who was so well-known that his name appeared in the dictionary, my story was much like that of other women. It was a search for my own identity, a struggle to be my real self, not what others expected me to be. At mid-life Hank was traveling all over the country and was treated like a media star. Our marriage began to fall apart. I had reached a point of despair when an event occurred that altered my life. I discovered alternative medicine.

My first discovery was a system of medicine called homeopathy, virtually unknown then in the United States. The result was a book I coauthored, *Homeopathic Medicine at Home*. Published in 1980, it has been translated into a half dozen languages and continues to sell all over the world. A second book, *What Your Doctor Won't Tell You*, came out in 1990 and introduced alternative medicine to thousands of Americans.

After so much time, even the thrill of discovering new medical treatments began to pall. I yearned to write about my family and my own life. I was flooded with memories, some comforting, others painful.

At first I ignored this new voice whose message threatened to interfere with my role as researcher and writer. I kept thinking, *Holistic health is where I made my reputation. How can I give up this hard-fought identity for something as risky as writing a personal memoir?*

A struggle ensued. My publisher was hounding me to update *What Your Doctor Won't Tell You*. So was my literary agent. I wanted to hang on to the niche that had given me acclaim and pleasure. At the same time, I wanted the more difficult task of understanding what lay beneath my parents' privileged existence. The urge to tell this story won out. I do not regret it.

—*Jane Murray Heimlich, winter, 2010*

1

Meet the family

Family secrets

The young wife and mother, Kathryn.

Kathryn seemed

to have everything.

She was pretty, she

had beautiful clothes,

and she was married

to a successful man.

But it wasn't enough.

One night in September of 1930, my father heard shouts and commotion outside on the lawn. He put down the advertising copy he was working on for the dance studio. He raised the window. Police sirens wailed, a hospital ambulance flashed light. He leaned out the window for a closer look. Three stories below, he saw his young wife's crumpled body stretched out and unconscious on the grass.

Mother awakened in darkness to find herself in the Mount Vernon, New York, hospital. "For days I lay flat on my stomach while Arthur brought up a parade of specialists to examine me," she said. When Dr. Benjamin Farrell, a white-haired surgeon, arrived to assess her condition, Mother said, "I had confidence in the sound of his voice and the sure gentle touch of his fingers."

Later, Dr. Farrell performed a three-and-a-half-hour operation to repair my mother's fractured spine. The details were truly bone-chilling. Dr. Farrell's technique, called a fusion, involved removing the little knobs on the spine with instruments resembling a hammer and chisel. The pieces were chopped fine and those bits of bone were placed along the broken segment. Even after the operation was safely over, Dr. Farrell said it would be weeks before they knew if my mother would ever walk again.

Afterward, things returned to normal—given the latitude of the word, however.

No one could have imagined that thirty years later, Mother, by then a television star, would engage in such daredevil stunts as swinging from a chandelier or being tossed about by an acrobatic troupe. She could have been crippled for life.

I was only 4 years old when my mother jumped out of the window of our third story apartment. She was 24, just twenty years older than my twin sister, Phyllis, and I. My only distinct memory of this event is of Phyllis and me walking down the hospital corridor hand in hand with Helen, our nurse.

For several weeks, my mother was encased in a rigid brace that extended from her shoulders to her hips. I don't remember whether she tried to lift her head to kiss us. I don't remember if she told us when she was coming home. I don't remember anything that took place in this hospital room.

Phyllis doesn't remember any of this, either. In fact, Phyllis told me that she first learned about the suicide attempt reading Mother's book, *My Husband, Arthur Murray*, published in 1960, thirty years later. Likely, the suicide attempt was kept quiet by my parents. My father would not have shared his concerns with us or even addressed any of our concerns. So our own lives went on as if nothing had happened.

Helen wheeled us around the estate grounds that once belonged to wealthy

James A. Bailey, who made his fortune as owner of Barnum and Bailey Circus. The Park Lane, where we lived, had been built on that beautifully landscaped property at the corner of Lincoln and Columbus Avenues in Mount Vernon.

Our apartment, like the others in the building, was luxurious. It boasted a wood-burning fireplace, spacious rooms with high cathedral ceilings, and a cheerful sun porch where Phyllis and I played, oblivious of my mother's increasing desperation. With a stunning apartment to live in, a successful husband, and a nurse to care for her four-year-old twins, how could she have wanted to kill herself?

It wasn't until recently that I uncovered a few clues. I talked with Dick Clark, who grew up playing in the sandbox outside the Park Lane with Phyllis and me and who later became a well-known TV star. Dick's parents, Julie and Richard Clark, were my parents' closest friends in the building. We children were constantly in and out of each other's apartments.

He had some startling insights about life at the Park Lane in the 1930s. The roaring good times of the young married set that the Murrays and the Clarks belonged to sounded like a page from F. Scott Fitzgerald. Dick recalled a constant round of parties. "They played cards every Friday. They all drank considerably. I've heard wild stories about the goings-on."

My mother loved parties. She liked the audience that gathered when she launched into one of her vaudeville songs; she liked the smile on her husband's face when she performed. She also liked the mugs of gin that, I suspect, lifted her depression, at least temporarily. These were the days of bathtub gin, when large quantities of cheap grain alcohol were mixed with a flavoring agent, such as juniper berries, to cut the taste. The taste, I'm told, was awful, like that of turpentine.

I know that my father didn't join the gin drinkers at the Park Lane. Arthur's mother, Sara, had no use for alcohol. None of Sara Teichman's offspring drank. My father was always on guard for signs that Mother was consuming too much alcohol. When my father was in a playful mood he'd say, "Liquor never did nobody no good." But more of the time he would lash out at my mother for drinking too much. Even in their later years he would look over at Mother, "Madam, you've had enough," and Mother, with a contrite smile, would push away her wine glass.

It was after one of those wild party nights that Mother attempted suicide. I believe it all began in the apartment kitchen. There, on one wall was a dumbwaiter that delivered food and dishes between floors. On the opposite wall, a window looked out on grass and shrubbery three stories below. It was an ordinary window on a level with the top of the kitchen table. This window haunts me even today because it certainly figured in her suicide attempt.

In her book my mother describes the suicide attempt quite differently than I imagined it. ". . . we had returned from a picnic . . . I can remember drinking homemade wine—not much, but even one drink makes me misty-headed. Feeling sick when we got back to our apartment, I went into the bathroom and locked the door . . . The window was rather high up and small. I must have climbed up on a chair, opened it, and jumped out."

This didn't jibe with what Dick Clark told me. He indicated that his mother was in the same room as mine. "Your mom and my mom were tiny women. My mother was barely five feet tall. Your mother tried to throw herself out of the window. My mom tried to stop her. My mother was there trying to pull her back—but she failed."

I assumed this took place in the kitchen. If Mother was tipsy she wasn't apt to climb up on a chair and jump out of a high small window. And what was a chair doing in the bathroom? Mother's version of the happening didn't ring true.

It was 1926, and Kathryn presented Arthur with twin daughters. She appears somewhat surprised by her accomplishment.

At a time when a married woman's success was measured by her husband's accomplishments, Kathryn Murray seemed to have everything. She had a successful husband who at the time of their marriage, in 1925, had taught more than five million Americans to dance by providing instruction through the mail. As a result of her husband's financial success, she had an immense wardrobe of beautiful clothes that Arthur had selected. Furthermore, she was the mother of what she called "curly headed darlings," whose antics my father recorded in endless reels of film.

In fact, they once invited a film producer to see home movies. After several hours of watching the twins playing in the sand box and with their dolls, the producer sneaked out under cover of darkness.

All in all, Kathryn Kohnfelder Murray from Jersey City, appeared to be doing very nicely. So what possessed her to try to kill herself? Most likely, my mother, astute as she was, realized that my father's real world was not the twins or the Park Lane parties or even his young wife. My father had recently founded a dancing studio at 11 East 43rd Street. Nothing in his career, not even the television show that he would produce twenty years later, could match the excitement of his first studio. Kathryn had no part in this excitement.

One of the dance teachers described my father's role: "He was everywhere, supervised everything. He trained the new teachers, selected the dance music; he wrote ads, he designed the decor of the waiting room."

Part of the excitement of the studio was generated by the Arthur Murray teachers. Owing to the Depression and the scarcity of jobs in New York, society girls and Harvard graduates clamored to be Arthur Murray teachers. The women were like the Southern girls that Arthur had admired so much in Asheville. Learning to read, Phyllis and I pored over an early issue of the studio magazine, *The Murray-Go-Round*, which showed head shots of beautiful women teachers. Each had shining hair and most wore a string of pearls.

Phyllis and I knew that we could never aspire to being beautiful like the dancing teachers. "You can be cute," Daddy said. We didn't say anything but we knew that "cute" was second-best.

The studio attracted illustrious pupils, among them ex-presidents, governors, senators, and members of the Royal families of Europe. My father wrote a booklet, *The Secret of Popularity*, whose cover bore a mythical coat of arms that helped instill an aristocratic air. "Society people form a large part of Arthur Murray's patrons," read the promotional booklet. "To dance smartly, as society girls must, it is necessary to learn from well-bred teachers who were reared in an atmosphere of culture."

Kathryn had no place in Arthur's world of beautiful dancing teachers and distinguished pupils. Now and then, Mother, Phyllis, and I visited the dancing studio. We sat in the reception room, then decorated with sedate antiques and traditional English hunting scenes, and listened to a constant round of foxtrot, waltz, and rumba. A few minutes before the hour, a pretty woman approached the man seated next to me. "Ready, Mr. Peters?" she asked. Pupil in tow, she glided away in her ankle-strap shoes, and soon we three were the only ones left in the room.

My mother was not only an outsider at the studio. Worse, she felt useless at home. Helen, who had become part of the Kohnfelder family at 14, had subsequently come to work for my mother when Phyllis and I were born. She unwittingly usurped Kathryn's role. Though Helen didn't need her, Mother felt she should stay at home with Phyllis and me—in those days a woman only worked if she needed the money—

but with Helen taking charge of the apartment and the twins, Kathryn had very little to do. The exception was Thursday, "maid's day off."

Thursday morning, Helen, in her navy suit with the rhinestone cat pin on the lapel, kissed us goodbye. We clung to her. "Now you be good to your mother," Helen said sternly. "We will," we chorused weakly. For a moment, Kathryn sat alone at the kitchen table and looked dolefully out the window. It was the same window that had figured in her suicide. Was it nice enough to take the girls for a walk? Unused to a motherly role, perhaps she worried about what she could do with us that day—how she would cross busy Columbus Avenue holding our little hands tightly, afraid that one of us would squirm out of her grasp. I know she must have fought off a feeling of despair. Everyone in the family agreed that no one could manage children as well as Helen.

Given the fact that women instructors were graceful creatures trained to execute the demanding footwork of a Viennese waltz or move to a sensuous tango. Given the fact that my father was totally dedicated to the studio. Given

If the new parents appear a little uneasy with this doubling of familial responsibility, they may be forgiven.

the fact that Mother was an onlooker at the studio with no part to play. Given the fact that I know the players so well, I've put together a scene that's very real to me.

One Thursday, on Helen's night off, when Phyllis and I were finally bathed, fed, and tucked into bed, Kathryn set the dinner table for two using her good silver candlesticks, monogrammed linen place mats, and napkins. It was a short walk for Arthur to get from the studio to Grand Central, a thirty-minute train ride to Mount Vernon. Since the studio stayed open until 10 and something always claimed my father's attention, he rarely arrived home before nine o'clock. This night he had promised to take an earlier train. It wouldn't hurt to remind him. She straightened a candle with a smile of satisfaction, and called the studio.

"Mr. Murray, please."

A minute later: "Dear, I have such a nice dinner . . . "

But the voice on the other end belonged to Catherine, the studio operator.

"I'm sorry, Mrs. Murray, Mr. Murray is dancing with Miss Eaton. May I leave a message?"

"No, thank you." She put down the receiver, her heart pounding. Miss Eaton is from Charleston, a Southern beauty. Kathryn recalled her trilling laugh. Miss Eaton wore gauzy dresses, an expensive French perfume. Once Arthur suggested that she go shopping with Miss Eaton. "She has excellent taste," he said.

Forty-five minutes later, Kathryn greeted her husband with a forced smile. She asked numerous questions: "Was the train crowded, how was the teachers' meeting?" And then, the smile intact: "Is Miss Eaton the best dancer in the studio?"

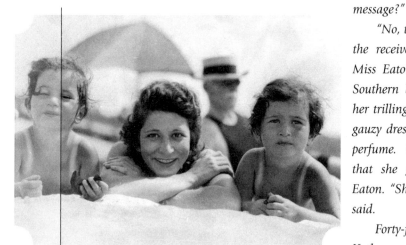

The girls at the beach at Castle Harbor in Bermuda. From left, Phyllis, Kathryn, and Jane.

Arthur pondered her merits. "We have a great many accomplished dancers. Miss Eaton's footwork is exceptional."

Kathryn continued the interrogation, her voice shaky. "You tell me you're so busy—why do you spend an hour dancing with Miss Eaton?"

Arthur frowned, annoyed at being questioned. "It is essential that I keep my dancing up-to-date. If Arthur Murray uses outmoded steps and ordinary styling, this will not attract pupils to the studio. Dancing is like any sport," he added. "It's essential that you practice regularly. Otherwise the leg muscles become weak . . . . "

Arthur continued describing the benefits of regular exercise while Kathryn sat, arms hugging her thin frame, a forlorn little girl who yearned to be taken into her daddy's arms.

It would take an extremely confident young woman not to feel jealous of the beautiful dancing teachers that my father held in his arms on the dance floor. Kathryn, who at 22 could belt out "Frankie and Johnny" and recite all ten verses of *The Shooting of Dan McGrew*, had a fragile self image. Photographs taken of my parents on their shipboard honeymoon show a pert, diminutive, extremely pretty brunette. Nevertheless, Mother persisted in describing herself as "an ugly duckling."

"I was a sallow, tiny, dark-haired child—always the smallest of the group—always the homeliest." Writers described her admiringly as a "petite bundle of energy." In reality, she hated being short. She called herself "runt, a midget, a dwarf" and blamed her size on her mother withholding milk when she, Kathryn, developed eczema as an infant.

"See?" she would say to perfect strangers, thrusting out a hand with long fingers and painted nails. "This mitt is as big as yours." My mother was convinced that her large hands indicated that she was meant to be taller than she was.

Kathryn's unloving relationship with her mother, Lenore, played a crucial part in her feelings of inferiority. Lenore was an auburn-haired beauty with thick hair that Phyllis and I, as small children, loved to comb by the hour. Her hips had a generous curve made fashionable by Lillian Russell. According to Helen, Lenore only thought about herself. "You should see the clothes in her closet. She never buys anything pretty for Kathryn."

Years later, Helen, quick to sense injustice, still glowered telling Phyllis and me how our grandmother favored Kathryn's older brother, Norman. "Norman did this, Norman did that," she mimicked.

In later years, Kathryn made a joke out of her mother doting on her son. "Norman learned to walk at six months," she said dryly. "He translated *The Iliad* at one year."

With Lenore's attention focused on Norman and her own good looks, Kathryn turned to her father, Abe, for love and affection. Abe, whose full name was Abraham Lincoln Kohnfelder, was a clever newspaper man, the advertising manager of the *Jersey Observer*, who had a brief stint in vaudeville until, as Kathryn quipped, "he decided he liked to eat."

Even here, she was less than fulfilled, for his remarks to her were frequently hurtful. "He would say, 'Well, kiddo, when you were born you sure were a homely little jigger,'" she recalled. "'One look at you and I went out and got drunk!'" He was not aware of the longing for approval in his daughter's nature, neither did he consider that a joke about a baby would hurt her feelings.

Still, his warmth and his maleness were enormously appealing to her. Abe taught his daughter World War One songs, and the two of them performed like a vaudeville team. Toward the end of her life, I taped Mother singing a dozen of these songs in a nasal voice that still had shades of New Jersey.

"When Frances Dances with Me" was my favorite. "He takes me to dances 'cause that's what I love; I fit in his mitt like a motorman's glove." But Abe, clever as he was, provided shaky emotional support for Kathryn. With the ex-vaudevillian, it was anything for a laugh.

More destructive than hurtful jokes was the danger of having your father as a role model. A therapist friend told me this is not a healthy arrangement. We learn how to be women emulating our own mothers. With my mother playing favorite roles, such as the little tramp, she never exuded a sense of womanliness. My mother never felt beautiful. Things had to be done to you to make you beautiful.

I imagine that another difficulty in her marriage to Arthur was that Kathryn was accustomed to a family that demonstrated their affections. Kathryn's father kissed his wife goodbye in the morning and kissed her when he returned at night. I remember my grandfather's hugs, which smelled of cigars and pipe tobacco.

By contrast, my father was raised in a loveless family that never hugged each other. The coldness carried over to his own family. He offered his cheek for a peck when we parted and we pecked a kiss on his cheek when we returned.

Even when we were 8 or 9, my mother still appeared to be looking for affection. I remember a Sunday afternoon when our parents, Phyllis and I had just returned from a walk around our suburban neighborhood. The sun poured in the windows of the wood-paneled library. Our coats hung up, my mother turned to my father and held out her arms beseechingly, like a little girl. He needed to be reminded. Then my father obligingly put his arms about his petite wife and they hugged.

Over the years I've tried to fill in the missing pieces of that fateful night. This is the scene that grew in my mind. It's as close to the truth as I'll ever come.

Kathryn rushed in from a party at the Clarks' apartment next door, Julie following. "I'll make some coffee," Julie said, keeping a worried eye on Kathryn. Arthur had just gotten home from the studio.

"Arthur, I'm sho glad you're home," Kathryn said. "Julie and . . . and . . . "
—she stammered, trying to recall Richard Clark's name—"will be sho glad to see you."

She frowned. "Why are you taking off your jacket?"

Arthur continued hanging up his gray suit jacket. "I have no desire to go to the Clarks' party."

"They"ll be so hurt."

"Nonsense."

"Yes, they will."

"When people are drinking they don't care about anything but liquor."

Uncomfortable at being involved in a quarrel, Julie left the room.

"Arthur, I promised to sing 'Frankie and Johnny.' I'll be home soon."

"Do as you please. I'm not interested in these people."

"Arthur, please don't be so mean."

"Kathryn, I've asked you to stop drinking but you don't listen to me." Then Arthur *disappeared into his study.*

When Julie returned, she found Kathryn standing on the kitchen table, the window open. She grabbed Kathryn, struggled with her but she was not strong enough to restrain her.

A minute later, Arthur heard shouts outside on the lawn. He leaned out the window and saw Kathryn, three stories below, stretched out and unconscious.

Why did my mother want to kill herself?

My daughters once asked me this question.

They were astonished that we had never consulted a therapist. "But didn't you ask your mother why she was so unhappy?"

I had to admit I had never discussed the subject. "In those days you never questioned a parent," I said lamely.

My daughters were unaware that their grandmother's suicide attempt at 22 was not a lone happening. The second attempt occurred three decades later in 1960. This time I was 34 and closely involved in the incident.

I think I have the answer to my mother's behavior but it's still a guess. Like so many secrets in our family, we never discussed it.

CHAPTER 2

The dancing
missionary

The maestro, at work.

Dancing lessons weren't

always confined to the studio.

Sometimes they came

home. We weren't the

best students, though.

Our minds—and feet—

wandered.

14

This evening was a state occasion. My twin sister and I, aged 8, were to have dinner with my parents in the dining room of our white colonial house in Harrison, New York. To get ready, we slipped into our dark green velvet dresses with lace filigree collars. This was a rare opportunity to share our triumphs and adventures with our parents.

Because the dancing studio in Manhattan stayed open until 10 p.m., my father generally had a late dinner with my mother when he got home. Phyllis and I ate in the kitchen with Helen.

This evening the four of us were seated in the dining room surrounded by walls papered with scenes of the landing of the Pilgrims. My parents sat at either end of the table, Phyllis and I on either side.

First, it was dance lessons. Then, with the Depression, it was economics lessons.

Crystal goblets gleamed in the candlelight. With my middle finger I made a ping sound on my goblet. Mother shook her head, then smiled at me to show she wasn't angry. Bertha, in a maroon-colored uniform, frilly white apron and cap, quietly removed the gold-rimmed plates that were used for show.

I was bursting to tell my news. A story I wrote about a little girl on the prairie was printed in the school newspaper. My teacher, Mrs. Whiteside, asked me to submit another story to the paper. David Guernsey chased me at recess.

I giggled, remembering my remark in class that day. Mrs. Whiteside was explaining what "habit" meant.

"Habit means doing something the same way each time. For example, what foot do you put your sock on first?" she asked.

The class pondered her question.

I raised my hand. "The cold foot," I said.

Even Mrs. Whiteside laughed.

I started to tell my joke at the table. But my father had launched into his favorite subject—the pupils whose lives he had changed by teaching them to dance.

"You remember Miss Peters?" he asked my mother. "She was so painfully shy. You should have seen her tango exhibition at the tea dance." Next, he described Mr. Thompson, once stiff and ungainly, who had become a graceful dancer, brimming with confidence.

Miss Brown. Mr. Malloy. More pupils and their stories. I felt as if the dining room was populated by these strangers, dancing round and round the table. But what about *me*? No one wants to hear my stories. I sniffled back my tears, then buried myself in the familiar scene of the Pilgrims offering beads to the Indians. Bored, Phyllis and I gave each other harmless pinches under the table. Like crickets, we rubbed one black patent leather Mary Jane against another to emit a faint squeak.

What I was too young to appreciate was that my father was his own best example of the transforming powers of dancing. Born Moses Teichman, his parents Yiddish-speaking immigrants, he was raised on New York's teeming Lower East Side. Arthur was a tall, gangly adolescent with a bad stammer. Joining a class in ballroom dancing at a neighborhood settlement house, he became an outstanding dancer and was on his way to carving a successful career.

My father, always immersed in the present, rarely talked about his deprived childhood. It was my mother who evoked our sympathy for a frequently stern father. The history lesson usually began with our hurt feelings. We rushed to Mother, wailing, "Daddy's so mean." Mother gathered us on the chaise lounge in her bedroom. She took a deep breath.

"Your father was a very poor boy." She paused. "He did the family ironing. He was so poor that his mother couldn't spare a penny for him to buy candy." We are spellbound, close to tears although we have heard this story many times before. By the end of the recital, Scheherazade has woven a spell that sends us happily back to our room to play jacks.

The dancing studio was like a body of water that only occasionally lapped at the shores of our suburban island. One of these unusual occurrences was a dancing lesson that, in the early 1930s, my father gave on the radio every Friday evening. The lesson became part of our structured routine.

At five o'clock, Helen turned on our RCA radio, which stood imposingly on the top shelf of the bookcase. First, we listened to *Jack Armstrong, the All-American Boy*, followed by *Dick Tracy* and *Buck Rogers*. This allowed fifteen minutes for our bath before Daddy's program, which aired at 6 o'clock. Despite Helen's repeated threat, "You'll miss your father's show!" we dawdled, squeezing our rubber ducks. The announcer's voice came on.

"And now it's time for your weekly dancing lesson."

"Quick!" Helen commanded.

We climbed out of the tub with much splashing, dampening the tub mat. Then, swaddled in towels, we scrambled to stand in front of the radio set.

"Today, I'm going to teach you the box step," my father said in his high-pitched voice. "Men start with the left foot stepping forward. Women start with the right foot stepping backward. Gentlemen, ready with your left foot."

Then in a singsong voice: "Forward, side together. Back, side together." We giggled uncontrollably as we struggled to execute the step.

"Daddy said *backside*, Daddy said *backside*."

"Hush," Helen hissed, "you're missing the lesson."

Since we had little interest in learning the basic dance steps, my father decided we should learn to tap dance. Our teacher was Gloria Hatrick, who later married actor Jimmy Stewart.

One Saturday morning, Miss Hatrick, a tall, handsome, outdoorsy woman, arrived at our house. We shyly led her to the library where the rug had been rolled up. Our Mary Janes were slippery. We began with the waltz clog as Miss Hatrick showed us the basic step. We tried to do it but without much success. She demonstrated the step again and again singing, "East side, west side." We promised to practice.

The following Saturday, we added arm movements to the waltz clog and a little "styling." The following week, Miss Hatrick showed us a new routine that ended with a lunge and an outstretched right hand. "Girls, raise your eyebrows on the lunge step, flirt with your audience." Phyllis and I looked at one another. We felt silly.

After a few more sessions, Daddy told us that Miss Hatrick would not be here this Saturday. Did she think we were too dumb? Was the commute too long? We never asked.

My father once said, "I don't sell dancing— I sell popularity." An ad that promised "How I Became Popular Overnight" attracted 37,000 replies.

My father's missionary zeal proved ineffective at encouraging us to learn to dance. So next, he turned to a lesson in how to make money. It all began with our favorite plaything—a miniature store from FAO Schwarz. Displayed on the tiny counter next to the cash register was a stack of crisply folded white shopping bags, with the imprint "J & P," a play on the A&P stores, which were rapidly emerging as supermarkets in the 1930s. The shopping bags were furnished by my grandfather Abe, the advertising manager.

We might have been satisfied to play store with the tiny make-believe cereal boxes and other inedibles but my father stepped in with a more dynamic idea. "Why don't you run a real store?" he suggested. "You can buy supplies at a lower rate than you sell them. You'll make a good profit."

We weren't quite sure what my father was talking about but we were thrilled to have his attention. Wasting no time, Daddy drove us to Seligson's stationery store to launch our merchandising venture. He picked up three Baby Ruth bars. "Here, they're offering three candy bars for ten cents. You can sell the candy for five cents apiece." Our minds whirling, we nodded, trying to keep it all straight.

There was no problem finding customers for our merchandise. Our parents frequently invited Arthur Murray couples to spend the weekend. When they arrived, we flashed winsome smiles and invited them to visit our store. There the hapless guests stocked up on toothpaste, shaving cream, chewing gum, and other items.

During this transaction, our shiny black cash register chimed merrily. Later, coins that were collected from the bottom compartment of the cash register were dropped into a piggy bank. Eventually, we deposited our earnings in a savings account at the Harrison bank. We handed our slim savings book, maroon with the name of the bank in gold writing, to the teller. Under the gaze of two pairs of eyes, the teller painstakingly wrote in blue ink the amount of our deposit.

One day in March of 1933, we heard our parents talking in worried voices. "They call it a bank holiday," my father said grimly. "I hope he knows what he's doing." As we learned shortly, my father was referring to President Franklin Delano Roosevelt closing the banks all over the country.

Here, under the watchful presence of Father, Phyllis and I work on the coordination of hand and eye, as opposed to the feet.

Phyllis and I looked at one another. I said to her, "What's happened to our bank account, our store money?" I ran to the bedroom to fetch my savings book to show my father.

"Have they taken our money? Is there no more money in the bank?" I asked worriedly.

Daddy shook his head. "The bank's closed. FDR closed the banks."

"But what's going to happen to all our store money," I wailed.

Daddy shrugged. "We've all lost a lot of money," he said with a wry smile.

Lost a lot of money! I ran to my favorite hiding place underneath the kitchen table. My heart was pounding. *We're going to be poor, we're going to be poor. I'll sell newspapers.* I visualized myself tugging at my wool cap like Jackie Coogan and blowing on my cold fingers. *I'll bring home all the money I earn and buy food for everybody. Then we'll eat in the kitchen on an oilcloth tablecloth and have dinner together every night.*

I don't remember whether we recovered our store savings or not. But our family's life remained unchanged. At age 7, I was as secretive as ever about the dancing studio. Our friends' fathers were lawyers or businessmen. On weekends they went skeet shooting or played golf. They didn't listen to tango music or make up dances such as "The Big Apple."

The dreaded encounter between my father's world and ours occurred one Saturday when I invited my best friend, Margaret, over to play. As we walked past the living room, I heard the strains of "Tony's Wife," a rumba, coming from the Victrola. And then, to my horror, there was my father dancing around the uncarpeted edge of the room wiggling his hips and looking very serious. I knew what he was doing. Earlier that year, he and my mother had traveled to Cuba to investigate the new Latin dance, the rumba. As they discussed endlessly at the dinner table, the rumba dancing was spectacular. But the question taunted my father: *what made the hips move in that sensuous undulating fashion?* When he asked the Cuban dancers, all they could do was shrug their shoulders and say, *Observame!*

That explanation didn't satisfy my father. He needed to analyze a dance in order to teach it. But thus far, the secret of rumba motion eluded him.

"Let's go," I said tugging Margaret's arm, but she refused to budge. My father by then had turned off the music. He placed his hands on his hips and was slowly ascending the front stairs. He paused, one foot on the next step. Then he took another step and his hips swung in the opposite direction. We were witnessing a Eureka moment!

"Madam!" he bellowed up the stairs. (He used a shortened form of Madam Big Boss, his favorite name for my mother). My mother, Kathryn, came running down.

"The secret of the rumba motion is where you place your weight," he said, his stammer more evident with his excitement. "Take a step with your left foot and place your weight on your right. Your hips naturally swing to the right. Now take a step with your right foot and your hips swing to the left."

My mother gave my father a worshipful look. They tripped down the stairs to the living room. He wound the Victrola again, and soon the two were dancing around the room, their hips undulating from side to side.

In our family, "introvert" was a much despised word, so I worked very hard at being Miss Sparkle Plenty (at right). I succeeded pretty well, particularly when I was with my sister.

Later, Daddy asked us if we wanted to learn the secret of rumba motion. "Yes," we said, obediently. We stood at the bottom of the front staircase and put our hands on our hips.

"Now take a step with your left foot."

I thought about Margaret. *Will she tell the kids at school?*

My father gave me a sharp look. "No, the weight remains on the right foot." He looked annoyed. "You're not paying attention. I'm wasting my time."

"Daddy," we protested, fearful of his disapproval, but he was already ensconced in his armchair, his reading glasses perched on his nose.

Years later, after we graduated from college, my father suggested that we teach dancing for a year. "You will improve your dancing and acquire grace and confidence," he said. We had no other job proposals so, without much enthusiasm, we agreed. After several weeks of training, we became Arthur Murray teachers. Not wanting to be known as Arthur Murray's daughter, I appropriated my college roommate's name, Joan Ogdon.

Before long, it was apparent that Miss Ogdon had a dismal sales record. My pupils liked me—they asked to work with me—but while other teachers induced their students to extend their courses, I rarely mentioned renewing their course of lessons. I explained to my supervisor, Miss Ray, "Mr. Smith's wife said he has a new baby on the way and they can't afford to spend money on dancing."

"What about Mr. Sinclair?" she inquired. "He just bought a house—he has a mortgage payment to pay," I countered.

Miss Ray picked up her teachers' manual, her lower lip trembling slightly. "You must believe in your product, Miss Ogdon. Dancing changed my life."

To my dismay, my sales record came to my father's attention. He sat on the living room couch, his lap heaped with letters. Waving a hand for me to sit down, he cleared his throat.

"Miss Ray tells me you don't wish to discuss renewing lessons with your pupils." He pulled out a slip of paper that recorded Mr. Sinclair's sales record.

"Daddy, I can't press him to take more lessons. He has a new house—mortgage payments are steep."

My father moistened his lips. How many lessons have you sold to that young man?"

I hesitated. "Maybe five."

"You have wasted that young man's money," he said. I held my breath. "Dancing is like any sport. You wouldn't expect to learn to play tennis in five lessons. The muscles need to be trained. It takes a great many lessons to learn to dance. But once the dance steps become part of you, you will evoke admiration and applause whenever you appear on the dance floor.

"Isn't that *your* story, Daddy?" I said.

"That's the story of any of our long-time pupils," he said crisply. "Anyone can become a beautiful dancer if he's willing to take the time and effort."

As much as I respected my father, I considered some of his pronouncements as laughable eccentricities. Dining at a restaurant, my mother, Phyllis, and I knew better than to sit down at the first table the captain showed us. Instead, we took our clue from my father, who, still standing, glanced upward at the ceiling air conditioning vent and raised his hand to determine that a breeze was blowing down on him. We restaurant nomads then continued our search for a draft-free table.

CHAPTER 3

Moving to Hollywood

Jane herself, and looking very 1940ish.

In the 1930s, my father took the family west, seeking a cure in the perpetual sunshine. It was a nice theory, but there were things even sunshine couldn't cure.

My father worried excessively about his health, although to my knowledge he had no health problems. Everyone in the household dreaded those mornings when he appeared, heavy-lidded in his brown Viyella bathrobe, and solemnly announced that "my pillow was wet last night," signifying night sweats, a sure prelude to a cold. With the advent of the first cold symptom, he immediately took to his bed, a thermometer jutting from his mouth at a jaunty angle, like the cigarette holder that Franklin Delano Roosevelt favored.

In 1938, when an X-ray revealed a shadow on his lungs, he decided to retire. He was 43. He feared that the shadow, which later turned out to be an innocuous scar, meant tuberculosis, the scourge of immigrant Jews on New York's Lower East Side where he grew up. He announced one evening at dinner that if he didn't have long to live he wanted to enjoy himself. Soon after, my parents told us that we were moving to Beverly Hills, known for sunshine, tennis, and celebrities. With lightning speed, we sold our colonial house in Harrison, New York, and prepared to move.

Phyllis and I were 12. Wearing our plaid jumpers, we sat on the apple green carpet of our yellow bedroom, engaged in the painful task of sorting books and toys before the move. Each of us had walnut wood beds with hand-carved railings and our names on the footboard; one post on my bed was a carved elephant I had chewed on as a baby. We parted reluctantly with books that Mother said we would never read again. I bid a sad farewell to our dozen volumes of the Bobbsey Twins series. We were too old for our Tootsietoy cars but after much deliberation decided to keep our ball and jacks.

One of the L.A. perks was spending time with Groucho Marx, kibitzing with the master.

I was dimly aware that our forthcoming move left Helen, our nurse, without a job or home. "What's Helen going to do?" I asked my mother. She took a deep breath and said Helen deserved a rest and she was going to find her a lovely apartment in New York. Helen, her lower lip jutting out, said she was going to find her own place. It didn't take her long before she discovered a third floor walk-up on First Avenue.

Mother made a last try. "Helen, you may not realize how much money you have."

Helen gave her former charge a withering look. "There's nothing wrong with that apartment."

The wrench of leaving Helen, my house, school, and friends was offset by the prospect of living in Beverly Hills, home of the stars. Phyllis and I had cut our reading teeth on movie magazines. In fact, my first attempts at writing were letters to the editor of *Photoplay*. "Please print more pictures of Shirley Temple. I do not like Jane Withers. She is a show-off."

We pored over articles in the magazine, observing headlines that grabbed our attention: "Are Clark Gable and Carole Lombard 'just friends'?" "Is Gary Cooper really shy?" "What makes Myrna Loy the perfect wife?" We gazed at photos of Jean Harlow, the platinum blonde in white satin lounging pajamas, Eleanor Powell in tails, holding the brim of her top hat. I could still feel the pulpy pages of *Silver Screen* and *Modern Screen* under my fingernails as we read about the stars—Joan Crawford and Franchot Tone, Barbara Stanwyck and Robert Taylor, Lana Turner and Errol Flynn dancing the night away at the Trocadero, Ciro's, and the Cocoanut Grove.

In June of 1938, our family took the Broadway Limited train from New York to Chicago where we boarded the fabled Super Chief. Barely two years old, "the train of the stars" had set a speed record of forty hours between Chicago and Los Angeles. Commercial airplanes were only beginning to pose competition. The new twin engine DC-3 flew coast to coast, making two stops in seventeen and a half hours, but flying in a "prop" plane was noisy and cramped.

One evening we boarded the train, surrounded by our luggage on the platform of the cavernous Dearborn Station in Chicago. Phyllis and I wore our navy blue suits with pleated skirts and tailored jackets about which Helen said "won't show the dirt." We promised her we would take a sponge bath every day and change our underpants.

The silver serpent, gleaming in the darkness, looked as though it were awaiting us. Finally, after the conductor's penetrating call, "All a-boarr-d," we climbed the stairs. Once inside, a porter, attired in a crisp white jacket, took us to our compartment and unlocked the door of the doll-sized interior. Meanwhile, our suitcases were stowed in the baggage car.

At 7:15, our streamlined train glided out of Dearborn Station. As it gathered speed, I looked out the window and saw a blur of tenement apartments. Soon we were charging through the suburbs of Chicago, the train's air horn bleating insistently.

A waiter, chimes in hand, who passed our compartment door, struck a gong and in a singsong voice intoned, "First call t'dinner." Phyllis and I dashed to the dining car, our parents trailing behind. We swayed from side to side as we made our way through the green curtained aisle of the Pullman car. Pulling open the heavy door of the sleeping car, we emerged into the open air where I was assaulted by the deafening clatter of metal wheels on rails. The platform shifted under my feet. My stomach lurched at the thought of losing my balance. I grabbed the handle of another door, opened it, and sprang to safety. Phyllis followed close behind.

Moving to Hollywood

After making our way through several cars, we arrived at the dining car and entered a prim oasis with rows of tables, each set with white linen and a single yellow rose in a silver vase. We were greeted by the head waiter, who bowed to our parents and escorted us to our table. I read the menu: "fresh crabflake cocktail, consommé, grilled Lake Superior whitefish, breast of capon à la king, sirloin steak with French fried onions." How could all those dishes have emerged from that tiny kitchen? Phyllis and I ordered lamb chops, which were dressed in white frilly ruffs. We fingered the deeply etched designs on the heavy silverware.

While we were at dinner, the porter magically turned our couch into two berths, one on top of the other. A sink with toothbrush holder and drinking glass hung from the wall. We each had our own blue-striped hand towel. Testing, I pushed the hot and cold faucet holders to release a stream of water that filled the bowl, sloshing precariously with the train's motion. After much deliberation, Phyllis agreed to let me have the upper bunk. Our parents were next door.

Early the next morning when the train screeched to a stop, I climbed down to the lower bunk. We lifted the window shade and stared out at a few lone figures on the platform and wondered if they could see us.

What bliss for movie buffs, strolling through Beverly Hills. They look like sisters, but the pretty girl in the middle is their mother, Kathryn. (Jane at left, Phyllis at right.)

Later, we spent hours in the club car, mesmerized by the wheat fields rushing by. We knew from the map that we were in Kansas, on our way to New Mexico. Lightheaded from the smell of cigars, we clicked the ice in our highball glasses. My tongue tingled from the peppery ginger ale.

One of our companions in the club car was a stout older man whose vest buttons strained at each opening. "I'm on city council so I can tell you anything you want to know about Beverly Hills. What did you say about Lana Turner? No, I don't know where she lives." He cleared his throat. "Beverly Hills is a fast growing town with a population of 30,000. Make sure your parents take you to see the electric fountain at Wilshire and Santa Monica Boulevards.

You may want to go more than once." Two days later, orange groves appeared as we neared Los Angeles.

According to dancing star Ann Miller, "it was the very best of the tail end of the golden era" that began in the early 1920s. "You'd walk into Romanoff's and see everybody!" she wrote. "People like Louis Jourdan, Leslie Caron, Erroll Flynn, Humphrey Bogart. It was wonderful!"

The Marx family and the Murrays at a dude ranch in Palm Springs, California. From left: Phyllis Murray, Miriam Marx, Kathryn Murray, Mrs. Perlman, Arthur Marx, Jane Murray, and Groucho.

Arriving at the Los Angeles Union Passenger Terminal, Phyllis and I put on our new harlequin sunglasses that made us feel like movie stars. We hopped into a taxi, driving along, craning our necks for a glimpse of Grauman's Chinese, the ornate movie palace where stars left their footprints in fresh cement. We gazed despondently at the shantytown clutter of downtown Los Angeles. The movie magazines had promised an endless landscape of glamor, a perfect place. I looked over at Phyllis's stony profile, knowing she was feeling as let down as I was.

After what seemed like hours of weaving through traffic, we emerged into the landscaped perfection of Beverly Hills. There, the sunlight bounced off Spanish style buildings the color of cornmeal. Towering palm trees, like leggy Copacabana show girls, lined the boulevards. "There's Ciro's," we nudged one another, thrilled to actually see the nightclub where we read that movie stars danced the night away.

"There's Armstrong and Shroeder's," we said in unison, which was known for its "little thin hot cakes," the billboard proclaimed. And wonder of wonders, we saw that the Brown Derby restaurant was only a block from our hotel.

Our taxi, a minnow in a stream of sleek limos, pulled up at the canopied entrance of the Beverly Wilshire Hotel, bedecked by a bower of yellow and orange mums and potted trees. An attendant in a fitted red coat and black top hat opened the door. Phyllis and I alighted as gracefully as we could, pretending that we were the British princesses, Elizabeth and Margaret Rose. The Beverly Wilshire, which had opened in 1928 and occupied a square block on Wilshire Boulevard, was then a luxurious apartment-hotel. In the room we picked up elaborate hotel literature and learned that the lobby was decorated with gilt clocks and cupids, Aubusson carpets, and sparkling cut glass chandeliers.

We took the ornate elevator to the penthouse, our new home. Giggling, we dashed down the hall to the living room, opening doors, shrieking at each new wonder. After Mother designated which bedroom was ours, Phyllis and I held up our fingers and played "rock, scissors and paper" to determine who got first choice of bed and bureau.

In the midst of unpacking, Mother said we had better have lunch before we got too hungry. "Please, *please* can we have lunch at the Brown Derby?" we begged our parents. They nodded and smiled. The celebrated restaurant was just as we imagined. On the roof perched an enormous brown derby hat. We stepped inside where we saw the brown leather booths we had read about. The walls in the background were hung with portraits of movie stars. We quickly recognized Clark Gable, Vivien Leigh, Greta Garbo, and James Stewart.

Seated in a booth at the back of the bustling restaurant was Fred MacMurray, who, as we knew from our reading, went from small-town boy to romantic lead with stars such as Claudette Colbert, Carole Lombard, and Katharine Hepburn. Autograph books in hand, we trotted fearlessly over to his booth. He looked up and smiled at us. Sure enough, there were the dimples and the thatch of dark brown hair. He signed our books and readily agreed to a photograph. Daddy signaled to the photographer, clicking his thumb and middle finger the way he summoned a waiter.

Back in our penthouse living room, I opened the leather-bound writing case on the desk and took out a sheet of stationery embossed with the hotel crest. Before we left New York, I had made a pact with my best friend, Margaret Whiting, to tell her about every movie star that I saw. "We saw Fred MacMurray," I wrote. "He has dimples and is very nice."

My next letter to Margaret began, "Joan Crawford talked to us!!!" This little-dreamed-of encounter took place at a premiere at Warner Beverly Theatre on Wilshire Boulevard. Phyllis and I, decked out in our polka dot organdy dresses, staked out a place in the lobby away from the crowds amassed on the sidewalk. Like an apparition from a fairy tale, Joan Crawford, dressed in a long, glittering, white, sequined gown and ermine wrap, alighted from a limo at the curb and floated up the red carpet.

She saw us, stopped, and bent down to talk to us. Being so close to that famous face, the enormous eyes, the wide red mouth, we were struck dumb. Years later, I thought of this encounter when I read that Joan Crawford had adopted twin daughters. One of the twins, Christina, later exposed her mother's fanatical neatness and abuse in *Mommy Dearest*.

Back home in Harrison, we rarely ate at restaurants. Like any conscientious suburban housewife, my mother prided herself on producing tasty home cooked meals. My father preferred going out to dinner. On one of our rare visits to a restaurant, my father looked around contentedly. "Isn't it more interesting looking at a roomful of people than staring at the wallpaper?" I liked our wallpaper that depicted the landing of the pilgrims and felt hurt.

In our new life, we ate out every evening. One of our favorites was The Cock N' Bull on Sunset Boulevard, frequented by members of the British film colony. In the dimly lit walnut wood interior we frequently spotted David Niven and Ronald Colman and their wives. A buffet table in the middle of the room held an immense roast beef glistening in the light from an overhead spot. The chef saved the natural juices for my father as Helen had done at home.

Another favorite restaurant was Dave Chasen's. On the way to our table, we passed the dim interior of the pine-paneled bar where liquor bottles gleamed like jewels in Aladdin's Cave. We breathed in rich smells of steak and cigars, scotch, and Arpegé perfume. One night, we saw Cesar Romero and George Burns and Gracie Allen. Back in our hotel room, we added their names to our list of stars who had signed our autograph book.

We applied for membership at the Beverly Hills Tennis Club and were quickly accepted. Unlike clubs back home in Westchester, New York, with clay courts, sloping lawns, and spacious club houses, the club was located on a side street among small offices and modest homes. The air surrounding the club had a burnt incinerator smell. Despite its unpretentious setting, the club attracted top-ranking tennis players, largely because it was owned by Ellsworth Vines and Fred Perry, both international champions.

A great many members were film writers, stumpy bald men with New York accents. Their wives were fixtures in the locker room, dabbing on pancake makeup with a sponge. I felt sorry for them; they seemed to have nothing to do but put on makeup. Women at the club lived in two different worlds. The club's tile floors resounded with the click of high heels as starlets in short shorts and Veronica Lake hairdos that hid one eye paraded about like gazelles.

The club boasted a handful of movie actors. I was startled to see Peter Lorre, known for his sinister roles. He was dressed in a bathing suit. His simian looks were accentuated by profuse chest hair and long arms. Silent film star Gilbert Roland, mustached and distinguished, played tennis attired in slacks called white "ducks." His aristocratic looking wife, Constance Bennett, cooly attired in a silk dress, watched her dashing husband from the club's second floor porch. Phyllis and I didn't dare approach her for an autograph.

It was at the Beverly Hills Tennis Club that we met Groucho Marx and his family. Groucho had given up tennis but enjoyed watching his son, Arthur, a ranked player, compete in matches. Groucho was then married to Ruth Johnson, a former chorus girl whom he met during the run of *Home Again*, an early box office hit that played at the Palace in New York. I could see vestiges of the beauty she had been. She had dazzling white teeth and deep set blue eyes accentuated with heavy blue eye shadow, but the orange pancake makeup failed to cover squint lines and wrinkles on her suntanned face. With the merciless eyes of the young, we noted a roll of fat on her thighs escaping from her short shorts.

The Marxes' daughter, Miriam, was 13, our age. A defiant tomboy, she appeared day after day in the same mismatched, faded, flowered shorts and shirt. By contrast, Phyllis and I wore white tennis shorts and shirts with a Fred Perry insignia on the breast pocket. Miriam's daring exploits made us uneasy. One day, fully clothed, she dived into the club's pool and began swimming laps, kicking ferociously. Another time, she boasted that she had spent the night sleeping on a rug in front of the fireplace in the rec room of her home with her beloved German shepherd, Duke.

"Your mother allowed you?" I asked.

"She's never around," Miriam said with a knowing smile.

By this time, we were almost daily visitors at the Marx home, a large comfortable Spanish style house on Hillcrest Drive. We soon learned that the Marx marriage was "on the rocks." Occasionally Ruth waved to us on her way out with a sandy haired dancing teacher named Larry, whose thin legs were perpetually sunburned. Miriam's older brother, Arthur, 18, reticent, with a smattering of acne, was seldom around. The Miriam we knew bore faint resemblance to the photo on the piano of her as a little girl, a smiling Shirley Temple look-alike in a ruffled dress.

It was Groucho who was the main attraction for us. The Marx Brothers movies were enormously popular in the 1930s. The best, according to his son, Arthur, who would later write *My Life with Groucho*, were *A Night at the Opera* and *A Day at the Races*. We had never seen any of the Marx Brothers' movies but we were thrilled to be in the presence of a real movie star.

Groucho was completely different from my father. Daddy was always fastidiously dressed. When he left home for the dancing studio, a mid-morning departure that we only rarely witnessed, he wore a dark London-tailored suit and vest, his round shirt collars fastened with a gleaming gold pin. Standing close to him, I could smell Guerlain's lemony Imperial cologne. Groucho, who usually dressed in rumpled corduroy slacks and flannel shirt, exuded maleness. His house was an intriguing masculine domain that smelled of leather furniture, cigar and pipe smoke, and men's wool sweaters.

Owing to dance studio hours, which were similar to a theatre, my father was rarely at home. Groucho was always around the house, amiably conversing with us, or singing and accompanying himself on the guitar. He had plenty of free time. The public had finally tired of the Marx Brothers' zany movie antics, and it was seven years before the first broadcast of the smash hit radio show, *You Bet Your Life*, which made Groucho famous in his own right. Being "at leisure" during this lull, Groucho enjoyed spending time with young people, his own children and others.

Sweet teenagerdom in Hollywood.
Part of the thrill was knowing that Shirley Temple had just bought the same dress.
(Jane, left, and Phyllis.)

Phyllis and I were a ready audience. We laughed hysterically over Groucho's bantering wit. At one point, I fell off the dining room chair in a fit of laughter. His favorite subject was how to tell us apart, which led to a doggerel, "Jane's the one without the mole," which he recited at a rat-a-tat pace. Sitting cross-legged on the carpet of his den, we looked up adoringly as Groucho strummed the guitar and, in his nasal twang, sang, "Lydia, the Tattooed Lady. She has eyes that folks adore so..." He worked his eyebrows up and down and leered . . . "and a torso even more so."

Another favorite song was "Ten Cents a Dance," the plaintive lament of a dance hall hostess. We sat in respectful silence as Groucho played a scratchy recording by Ruth Etting, a popular torch singer of the 1920s. Listening to Etting's high-pitched, achingly sweet voice, we felt worldly wise and sad, as if we shared the singer's romantic yearnings.

I envied Miriam having a father as playful and demonstrative as Groucho. He gave her bear hugs that she perversely wriggled out of. She reserved her affection for her dog, Duke, slobbering kisses on his mouth. In our family, we didn't hug.

Unlike Groucho, my father preferred the company of women to that of men and children. When attending a party, he would approach one of his women friends and with a courtly bow say, "That's a very becoming outfit."

Groucho was a man's man. He had a wide circle of men friends, unimposing looking, most with paunches filling out cotton shirts, and to my surprise I learned that these men had written dozens of hit songs and Broadway musicals. They were all nimble-witted ex-New Yorkers, as rumpled and brainy as Groucho. They included Morrie Ryskind, known best for co-authoring the screwball 1936 comedy, *My Man Godfrey,* and Norman Krasna, whose screenplays later included *White Christmas.*

Another was songwriter Harry Ruby, who wrote the music for several of Groucho's movies. He and Bert Kalmar had written "I Wanna Be Loved by You," which was sung originally by Helen Kane, the "Boop-boop-a-doop" girl, and later by Marilyn Monroe in *Some Like it Hot.* Ruby and Kalmar also wrote "Hooray for Captain Spaulding," which went:

> At last we are to meet him,
> The famous Captain Spaulding.
> From climates hot and scalding,
> The Captain has arrived . . . .

They wrote it for Groucho's movie *Animal Crackers,* then Groucho used it as the theme song for his television program. And now, I could hear Harry Ruby above the rest of the men. "Are you crazy?" he said, gesticulating with a cigar and punching each word. "You will never be adequately paid for your work in films. Never. They treat us like shit. They steal our ideas. Okay, okay. What am I doing here?"

He smiled benignly. "You can't beat the weather. Tell me something," he continued. "Where can you find a piece of good corned beef in this town? Greenblatt's? You must be kidding. What they sell is not corned beef. It's *bologna.*"

By this time, my mother's initial enthusiasm for Groucho had cooled. "He's a stingy S.O.B," she said to my father, and blamed Ruth's drinking on Groucho's belittling remarks. Each time Phyllis and I returned from a day with Miriam and Groucho, Mother sharply quizzed us about our activities. Her disapproval hit its peak when all of us, my parents and Phyllis and I, attended one of Groucho's parties.

After the guests had gone, I sat on the couch with Groucho and Phyllis, each of us contentedly rubbing one another's feet. Mother passed by and looked daggers at Groucho. On the way home, she could hardly contain her anger.

"Did you see that disgusting display?" she whispered to my father. "I am not going to allow those children to be exposed to that behavior." Her threat was meaningless because by then it was the end of summer and time for school to start.

Efforts to get us into Lakeside, a private school that Shirley Temple attended, were unsuccessful. I overheard my parents discussing the rejection. "They probably don't take Jews," Daddy said. Mother enrolled us in the eighth grade at El Rodeo, a public school at Whittier Drive and Wilshire Boulevard.

When I arrived on the first day, I was intrigued by the school's exotic exterior. The imposing Spanish style building had a bell tower just like a monastery. Walking inside, I was thrust into a scene unlike any I had known in school. I was overcome by the thundering clatter of feet up and down the stairs and the deafening babble of voices.

By the end of the morning, I knew I would never fit in. My clothes were all wrong. I wore my school outfit from Rye Country Day that consisted of a pleated plaid skirt with white cotton blouse buttoned onto the waist band. Girls at El Rodeo towered over Phyllis and me. They wore fuzzy angora sweaters and short cotton skirts, their hair set with bouncing curls. I was no match for their easy confidence and bantering boy-girl talk. They all had boyfriends and played Spin the Bottle at parties. I was used to tamer games like "punch board," played with a pick that punched out messages such as "Dance with a broom."

Phyllis bravely attempted to fit in. She wore dark brown lipstick, bought a pink angora sweater, and daringly applied a blonde streak to the hair above her forehead that was rolled in a pompadour. Mother was furious. "I am not going to take you out to dinner looking that way!" She didn't make good her threat but conversation at dinner was chilly.

I had only one friend, Marian Borun, whose father owned the Thrifty drug stores. She was exceedingly shy and spoke with a whispery voice. Her cashmere sweater sets showed off a soft, well-developed figure. She was unnaturally pale, a fact I connected with her being mysteriously excused from sports. We sat side by side in class, two misfits.

When I lived in Harrison, I had always loved school. I was the eager beaver waving her hand with the answer. It was a great thrill when Mrs. Whiteside, my beloved sixth grade teacher at Rye Country Day, read one of my compositions to the class. As she began, my heart pounded and I had to fight the urge to laugh hysterically at the sound of my own words.

At El Rodeo, it was considered square to be interested in school work. My home room teacher, Miss Diebold, a tall, sharp-featured woman, had Brillo-red hair and a raspy voice. During class, the kids passed notes and threw spitballs. The second week of school Miss Diebold kept me after class and told me to write a composition. After she read it, she confided that she wanted to see if I could really write a story.

"I thought you might have copied that story you wrote last week," she laughed. I was horrified. My teacher in Rye would never have thought such a thing.

We were now living in Alfred Hitchcock's apartment, a few blocks from the Beverly Wilshire on Wilshire Boulevard. Feeling a little uprooted by the move, we liked the novelty of living in a famous movie director's home. The living room overlooked a swimming pool, a rarity in those days. Owning a pool was a status symbol, like driving a Lincoln Continental.

One day, our entire class of El Rodeo eighth grade boys wearing swim trunks burst into the pool enclosure. Delighted that they were coming to see us, we watched them snapping towels at one another, diving in the pool, splashing and yelping. We quickly changed into our bathing suits and, eager to join them, ran down to the pool. Too late. No sign of their presence remained except mounds of soggy towels.

"Do you want to swim?" Phyllis asked me. I shook my head. It was clear by then that the boys had no interest in us; they just wanted to use the pool.

My parents shared our disillusionment with Beverly Hills. My father, bored with retirement, began spending more time at the Arthur Murray studio in Beverly Hills, one of the early franchise operations. Mother soon tired of taking tennis lessons and became critical of the glamorous Hollywood parties that had once seemed so exciting.

An incident that summed up Mother's feelings occurred the evening my parents attended a premiere of *Gone with the Wind* at Cathay Circle, one of the movie palaces. Fans crowded on either side of the canopied entrance. Klieg lights crisscrossed the sky. My parents strode up the red carpet, flashing smiles at either side. A woman clutching her autograph book, ducked under the cordon, and ran over to them. She peered up into Mother's face, then turned away in disgust. "Aw, you're nobody!"

After one year in Hollywood, we boarded the Super Chief and headed back to New York.

CHAPTER 4

Living with
an alias

Kathryn, Jane, Phyllis, and Arthur, posing for a New York newspaper.

As children, we were

not aware we were

Jewish. We joyously

celebrated Christmas,

and, soon, I even

invented for myself a

Waspish background.

Home from boarding school for Christmas vacation, I walked up the stairs leading to a brownstone apartment in Manhattan's East 70s. The wood door had a brass lion and was flanked by stone carvings. I opened the door where I was met by the blast of party sounds. I put on a name tag and looked for my hostess, Mrs. Loomis. She was the mother of one of my classmates.

Mrs. Loomis attempted to pitch her well-bred voice above the din of voices— "How delightful to meet you"—then peered at my name tag. I braced myself for the inevitable question which was not long in coming: "Are you one of the Long Island Murrays?" I shook my head, smiled, and quickly headed for the punch bowl.

I contended with this question at every social gathering. The embarrassment was that Murray wasn't my real name. As a young dancing instructor in 1916, my father changed his name from Moses Teichman to Arthur Murray. In those days, when anti-Semitism was rampant, shedding a Jewish name made sense. Quotas aimed at curbing the number of Jewish students were the rule at virtually every college. Help-wanted advertisements routinely stated that only Christians or Protestants need apply.

Despite the painful circumstances that caused a great many Jews to change their names, Daddy enjoyed poking fun at Jews with Gentile names. At a party when I was a teenager I watched with some trepidation as my father was introduced to a Burton Smith. I could tell from the mischievous glint in my father's eyes what was coming. "What was your name before Smith?" Daddy quipped.

It was a benighted time, when Jewishness was still regarded as a kind of handicap.

As a child, I was perfectly comfortable with the name Jane Murray. I didn't know I was Jewish. In the 1930s, Phyllis and I attended a co-ed private school, Rye Country Day School. Founded in 1869 for children of socially elite families, the school soon changed to an open admissions policy. Our class of forty students stayed largely intact from kindergarten through seventh grade.

Not surprisingly, at a time when realtors participated in a "gentlemen's agreement" not to sell to Jews and other "undesirables," there was not a single Jewish name in our class list. It didn't concern my sister and me that many of our classmates attended a Christian Sunday school. Instead of sitting through a boring service, we felt we were the lucky ones being able to play on Sunday morning.

All through grade school, I loved my name. I felt an author's pride seeing "Jane Murray, age 8" printed at the end of my latest poem in the "Poet's Corner" of the *Jersey Observer*. It was more than happy coincidence that my grandfather worked there. By the time I reached fourth grade, my byline appeared regularly in the *Rye Crop*, our grade school newspaper. An eager student, I was thrilled to hear my name when the headmaster announced the honor roll.

Jewishness was not a concern at this time. My parents' social lives were similar to their non-Jewish friends except for one unalterable fact of life: it was unthinkable for a Jew, celebrity or not, to be accepted as a member of a Gentile country club. My parents' response to this discrimination, like most other affluent Jews who scorned Jewish country clubs, was to equip their home with its own sports facility. We had our own paddle tennis court. We didn't have a swimming pool; few families did at that time. We learned to swim at summer resorts, and on warm days at home, we put on bathing suits to run giggling through the sprinkler.

One of the happiest times was Christmas. We celebrated Christmas as if it were our birthright. The season began with our poring over the FAO Schwartz catalogue and culminated in the magic of Christmas morning. Waking at an early hour, we struggled into our bathrobes and rushed down the stairs into the living room. There, beside the window, was an enormous tree glittering with bulbs and colored lights. I felt sorry for Bobby Eckhart, our next-door neighbor, who had a white tree and cold blue lights. Underneath our tree was a shimmering sea of gifts.

Through all the festivities, my father was a benign onlooker. Was he pleased with these Christian observances so at odds with his upbringing? Or was he secretly amused? I remember one time when Mother was going over her gift list and came upon a name that had been overlooked. "Damn," she said softly.

Observing her, he said, "You Jews worry more about Christmas than the Gentiles."

I can't remember how old my sister and I were when my mother told us we were Jewish. I also can't remember what provoked the disclosure, or how we reacted. Whatever the circumstances, this admission caused no change in family customs. There was no lighting of Shabbat candles on Friday night; no Passover dinners with gefilte fish, no Chanukah observances. I was barely aware that Jewish holidays existed. In college, I read about the Seder service and thought the word referred to a kind of cedar wood.

The awareness that we were Jewish did impart a sense that being Jewish was a handicap. It was akin to a deformity, like crossed eyes. My father's comment, "She looks Hebraic," evoked a dark clumsy girl with a prominent nose and a faint moustache.

Of course, something could be done to rectify the Hebraic nose. At age 16, my sister and I were taken to a plastic surgeon in Manhattan for a "nose job." We wordlessly looked at the surgeon's "before" photos whose subjects were clearly in need of improvement. I stole a glance at Phyllis. I couldn't see anything wrong with her nose. Nevertheless, without questioning or voicing any resistance, we numbly complied with our parents' wishes.

We were not alone. At that time, and continuing through the early 1970s, the rhinoplasty was a rite of passage, akin to orthodontia for Jewish teenage girls. My mother had already had her nose fixed, as well as a breast reduction. An engagement photo taken in 1924 shows a pretty 18-year-old with a rather long pointed nose. In a photo that appears in *The Murray-Go-Round*, a studio publication full of tidbits about celebrated pupils and dancing tips, her nose is short, giving her a pert look.

After the surgery, Phyllis and I spent two days in the hospital with bandages on our noses. When Mother visited us, she applied ice to the area around our eyes, which were black and blue. When we got home, we had to sit quietly and be careful not to blow our noses. A week later, when the bandages were removed, Phyllis's nose looked swollen. When I looked in the mirror on my closet door, my nose looked swollen, too. We didn't discuss our noses with each other. We were too angry at ourselves for not putting up a fight.

Years later, when I read a story in which a Chinese woman recalled having her feet bound, I felt the bottled up anger that we had never expressed.

Try as we might to improve our looks—according to Daddy's ideals—we knew in our hearts that we could never match the appearance of the real princesses, the Southern belles he had danced with in Asheville. They were graceful gossamer creatures who all seemed to be named Cornelia or Emily and who had blonde cornsilk hair and lilting voices. With brown hair and glasses, I could never be my father's little girl. But I never stopped trying.

The dark barely glimpsed world of my father's childhood in the slums of New York was not completely absent from our sanitized suburban life. Occasionally, on Sunday, we four drove in our black Lincoln to the Bronx to visit Daddy's parents. Grand Concourse Boulevard, the wide street with center island, showed vestiges of its once elegant past. We gazed at row upon row of uniform red brick apartment houses. I felt as if I were in a foreign country.

We climbed the stairs to my grandparents' second floor apartment, wrinkling our noses at the cooked cabbage and onion smells. Grandma opened the door. Their apartment was furnished with dark red chairs, doilies on the back, a fringed shawl on a drop leaf table. It was dark and stuffy. We kissed Grandma's cheek, which looked like a wrinkled walnut. She was tall and stern looking, her gray hair drawn back in a bun fastened with a tortoise shell hair pin. We nodded uncertainly at our grandfather, a small man in rumpled trousers and a worn sweater who was seated in an arm chair. He looked up from his newspaper, printed with mysterious black characters, and grunted a greeting. My mother drew up a chair near him.

"Papa, you're looking very well."

We can't understand his answer. Grandma served us *kichlach* (pronounced kick-el), large thick cookies with poppyseeds. We took a few bites, then hid the rest in our purses. We listened while our father and his mother conversed in Yiddish. Daddy sounded as if his mouth was full of food and saliva. I couldn't tell if they were quarreling or laughing. He talked so fast, in such an animated way, as if he had left his quiet self at home. I marveled at how this foreign language, kept underground like the hot springs we once visited, bubbled up, ready to use.

On the way home we whispered about the invitations that our friends in seventh grade received from Miss Elsie Covington to attend her dancing class on Friday afternoon at Christ Church in Rye. Dancing class continued through twelfth grade. Our favored classmates would also be invited to attend a cotillion at Christmas and one in the spring. Invitations to these parties were extended to Miss Covington's pupils who came from other towns in Westchester and Long Island. "It was a very snobby thing," a friend recalled.

Phyllis and I did not receive invitations from Miss Covington. We were only dimly aware of being excluded from dancing school. We weren't interested in boys, anyway. Weekends, we spent our free time climbing trees or playing outdoor games. Our parents never discussed the subject with us, but the rejection must have been a bitter pill for my father. In Atlanta in the early 1920s, mothers fought to have their children accepted in Mr. Murray's dancing classes.

In September of 1941, we attended Dalton School at 108 East 89th Street. As I learned later, Dalton had an impressive reputation as a "progressive school . . . focusing on the development of the whole child . . . " I wanted none of it. I yearned for the orderly world of Rye Country Day.

At my Rye school, at least to my knowledge, there were no Jewish children. Now, for the first time, most of our classmates were Jewish. One, Hope Goldberg, with a gleaming black pageboy, was as tall as a grownup. She invited us to watch Macy's Thanksgiving parade from her Central Park West sixth-floor apartment. It was a crisp sunny day. Walking to Hope's apartment I thought, *in Rye the kids are playing soccer.*

Hope answered the door wearing a two-piece knit suit, silk stockings, and pumps. She kissed us on the cheek the way adult women greeted their friends. We followed her into the living room. It looked as if it should be roped off, like a museum exhibit. We stepped gingerly onto the white sculptured carpet and paused to look at a mahogany breakfront with leaded glass doors. Each glass shelf had its own light, which shone on a china figurine.

"This is Meissen," Hope said. "My father collects Meissen." On the other side of the room was a grand piano bare of sheet music. Each gleaming wood table had its own crystal ashtray and silver lighter.

At the thumping sounds of a band, we sat with Hope in the bay window to watch the parade. Hour after hour, we looked down on the eerie sight of inflated balloon people marching to a steady hypnotic beat. I felt tongue-tied and uncomfortable. Hope chattered about a new lipstick at Bonwit's cosmetic counter. Hope's father joined us for a few minutes.

"That's some view, isn't it?"

We nodded. Hope's mother, wearing a Persian lamb coat and carrying an alligator handbag, kissed her daughter goodbye.

"Tell Gladys when you're ready for lunch."

Despite Hope's friendliness, we felt lost in New York. A more adventurous 16-year-old would have reveled in the treasures of the city—museums, concerts, theater—and explored the newfound freedom of traveling by bus or subway. Instead, I lay awake at night listening to the fearsome city sounds— the ambulance tearing through the streets, the incessant bleat of taxi horns—and yearned to hear the crunch of gravel on our driveway in Rye when our parents came home.

Would you wear a cheetah coat today? The Murray twins (Phyllis, left, and Jane) had no compunction about stepping out in 1942 wearing their furs.

Part of the problem was that we were accustomed to having our mother arrange our lives. But Mother had discovered the pleasures of a career and was working long hours at the dancing studio, her office side by side with Daddy's. Although boarding

JANE MURRAY
New York, New York

Entered: Class III; Editor-in-Chief of
Yearbook I; Dramatic Club II, I; Compass
III, II, Secretary I; Tennis Team III, II,
I; Old Girls' Play II, I; Green Team.
Where Found: INQUIRING AT THE "LOST
AND FOUND" WINDOW
Pet Expression: BUT WHY—I DON'T
UNDERSTAND . . .
Besetting Sin: FORGETFULNESS
Pet Hate: ROOM INSPECTION
Suppressed Desire: TO BE COOL, CALM,
COLLECTED AND ON TIME
Destiny: AN AUTHOR, HURRYING TO CATCH
A DATE LINE

Jane is a very bright girl—but puzzling! She writes amazing compositions, heads the Yearbook Board and the Compass—all without the slightest trace of efficiency.

Her drawers are littered with papers, half-written letters, salt and vitamin pills. She can find exactly what she wants by delving into stacks of overflowing notebooks, which are crammed full of bits of illegible scribble.

She writes terrifically amusing answers to all those men in Service—and then forgets to mail them. Her grades are high, but there is usually a red-crayon memo at the top of her papers: "Rewrite—legibly!"

Rooming next to Phyllis brings forth sisterly squabbles of, "Well, who bought that soap?" and "I sent the laundry out last week." When the corridor resounds, Jane assures everyone, "Why, we're just talking—we never argue."

Jane is so vague with that lovely smile—but she guides us with a firm hand. We wouldn't know what to do without her.

42

My page from the Shipley School yearbook of 1944. Editor of the literary magazine, editor of the yearbook, I was an eager student.

school was not a tradition in Jewish families as it was in well-to-do Gentile families, boarding school seemed a perfect solution for all of us.

When it was proposed by Mother that we go away to school, we were excited at the prospect. We had recently seen a movie with Jane Withers in which she attended a boarding school. Jane and her friends spent most of their time going back and forth to a nearby military academy. I envisioned myself riding on the back of a motorcycle, my arms around the waist of a cadet.

Mother, on the advice of a knowledgeable friend, chose the Shipley School in Bryn Mawr, Pennsylvania. Founded in 1894 by the three Misses Shipleys, the school, unlike the prevalent finishing school, was designed to prepare young women for college. It soon attracted a distinguished faculty; many had done graduate work in Europe. Besides its scholastic record, another inducement for my mother were the newly appointed headmasters, J. Russell and Mildred Lynes. A decade later, Russell became a literary celebrity as the author of *The Tastemakers*. He and his aristocratic looking wife, her hair drawn in a chignon, were an engaging but unlikely couple for the job.

In her interview with Mr. Lynes, Mother candidly volunteered that we were Jewish. Mr. Lynes, a boyish presence with sandy-colored hair, had assuaged any fears that we would not be welcome. "Shipley prides itself on scholarship," he said. "Your daughters have a very good record."

After a train ride from Penn Station to Philadelphia, from there the Paoli local to Bryn Mawr, we took a taxi to Shipley. The taxi pulled up at the main building, a dignified white Greek Revival house purchased in 1894. Inside a handsome door, to the left, was the Chinese room named in honor of four stiff and uncomfortable Chinese Chippendale chairs and several porcelain dishes on a shelf. Here, the boarder might receive her guest, provided that his name appeared on her visiting list. Another rule specified that "a girl may not introduce her brother to other girls in the school except by special permission from the Principals when the families are already acquainted."

We had already missed several weeks of school. Our first make-up session was with Miss Bohlen, who taught European medieval history. I soon discovered that Catherine Bohlen was a superb teacher. In her classroom the world of kings and queens and powerful cardinals and popes came to life amid the glamour of heraldry. The brilliant yellows and blues in a coat of arms dazzled the eyes. We mouthed our new color vocabulary—argent, azure, sable—and learned to recognize the mythical creatures, the lion rampant, the unicorn and griffin.

That first meeting with Miss Bohlen, Phyllis and I sat side by side in her high-ceilinged classroom. The glare of gray afternoon light streamed in the large windows that required a pole to open or close. Miss Bohlen wore a tweed suit, her thick legs shod in sturdy oxfords. She had a long horsey face with flaring nostrils, a mouthful of teeth like Eleanor Roosevelt. She stood at the blackboard, pointer in hand. She pointed to the Scottish Isles. "Here is where your ancestors most likely came from," she said in her emphatic accent that sounded English. We both hastened to correct the misunderstanding.

"Murray isn't our real name," we piped up together.

Miss Bohlen was at a loss for words. She had probably never had a Jewish student.

At Shipley, church attendance was required on Sunday morning. We had a choice of the Presbyterian or Episcopal Church, both imposing stone structures. This was our first experience attending any religious service. I liked the ritual of getting dressed up; in the spring, we wore straw hats and white gloves. I did not allow my lack of singing ability to deter me from singing every verse of a hymn, and with unflagging energy intoned the chorus, "Oh, hear us when we cry to Thee, For those in peril on the sea!" Sermons were gracefully worded and delivered in well modulated tones. One Sunday the Episcopal minister's subject was, "What the well-dressed Christian will wear." I occupied myself speculating on whether we'd have roast chicken or loin of pork for lunch.

Phyllis and I never discussed the fact that we were the only Jewish students at Shipley. We were much too busy forging our identities, each in our own ways.

I concentrated on grades; Phyllis became the class clown. We became proficient at keeping an impassive expression when any mention of Jews swirled about us. I was not so successful at controlling my tendency to blush at such moments.

At vespers one Sunday, held in the auditorium at five o'clock, a visiting clergyman delivered a sermon on tolerance. To illustrate, he cited the example of a civic-minded Jew in his community whose efforts were honored by members of the clergyman's church.

"These good people commissioned a bust of this Jew to be displayed in the vestibule of the church," he said as I felt the telltale flush spread from the back of my neck.

Another instance occurred one Saturday night. We girls in our bathrobes, arms clasped about our knees, sat on the floor of a room listening to Frank Sinatra on the radio. The crooner was then 27. Teenage girls fainted when he appeared at the Paramount Theatre in New York. After the program was over, Miss Hayes, the housemother on duty, reminded us in her tired Virginia speech that lights were out in twenty minutes.

"Yes, Miss Hayes," we chorused.

I felt at home in this cozy gathering until the more self-assured girls launched into telling jokes. Libby Reynolds, a sweet-faced girl from Pittsburgh, told a joke about Abie and Becky who were having trouble having a baby. I steeled myself for what was coming.

"'Vot are ve going to do,' Becky said. 'Ve vont a baby but'—a shrug—'no baby.' Finally, their neighbor, Mrs. Goldberg, comes to their rescue. 'Don worry. I'll tell you vot to do. You put your Long Branch in her Long Beach and you Rockaway.'"

In the darkness, my face burned.

My gifted English teacher was Miss Helen Young. Sandy hair drawn into a bun, her thin face pointed like that of a fox, she read our compositions aloud in her rich melodious voice. For the first time, I was getting a sense of my identity as a writer.

One day, she read a clumsy story about marriage, written by one of my classmates. "Dahling," she said in her Tallullah Bankhead voice, "I would suggest that you write about subjects in which you have some experience." I escaped her silky sarcasm that could reduce girls to tears. She prophesied that I was *New Yorker* material, a budding writer, and as graduation approached, I was the favorite for the English prize.

The day before graduation, I took the familiar gravel path—my measured steps denoting the solemnity of the occasion—from the main building to Miss Young's airy classroom. I saved this most meaningful farewell for last. Miss Young greeted me warmly, getting up from her desk. She sat at the desk next to me. She asked me about my college plans. I told her that I was going to Vassar, the college that Mrs. Lynes had selected for the honor students. She nodded approval. So many of her good students had gone to Vassar.

We chatted, smiling at one another. I saw another student waiting. "I better go . . ." I stood up and took a last look. Miss Young had a parting word for me.

"Dah-ling," she wrinkled her forehead in a mock frown. "Don't be too obsequious. You Jewish girls try so hard to please."

This incident so wounded me I invented my own ancestors. The summer I was 18, I attended summer school at the University of Wisconsin in Madison, idyllic at that time of year. Our brown-shingled residence house, nestled in pine trees, overlooked Lake Mendota. It was early that summer when I fell in love with David.

He was a New England Brahmin. He was tall and boyish, a graduate student in American history who spouted ideas like fireworks. A Shipley friend arranged our meeting. That evening we walked around the lake. I hurried to match his stride. We climbed a steep hill. The wind blew hard, flattening the pines. At the top, we stood, our arms about each other, savoring the wonder of our meeting.

After that, we met each evening at the Student Union. I sipped a beer and listened enthralled to this merry wordsmith. Sometimes, David's friends, a physics major named Carl and Carl's girlfriend, Kermit Roosevelt, joined us. David and I held hands. My heart thumped with happiness.

A rare moment when Arthur has time to chat with Jane and Phyllis.

One evening, David and I sat in outdoor chaise lounges on the scrubby lawn of the house where I lived. Fireflies flickered in the grass, an occasional plop resounded from the lake. David told me that his father was a college professor. I warmed to the image—suede patches at the elbows, his library spilling with books. Then the warning signal came: "He's very narrow-minded."

David explained that when the literary club his father belonged to accepted a Jewish member, his father resigned.

David broke the silence. "When did your family come to this country?" My mother had told me a few snatches about my father's parents. My grandfather was a farmer who came to this country to escape the pogroms in Austria.

"They were very poor," I began. "Life was so hard." And then I made a few alterations. "The potato crop failed. They had nothing to eat." A few more strokes and I had placed my forbears in the Irish immigration of the 19th century.

David didn't comment. We talked of other things. We lost touch after the summer. The following year I learned that David was engaged to be married. My mother saw the announcement in *The New York Times*. Years later, when I was happily married, my childish deception had the power to awaken me in the early hours of the morning. It has bothered me for a long time that I made up a story that denied my Jewish roots.

CHAPTER 5

Life in the spotlight

Kathryn and Arthur, all smiles whenever the flashbulbs popped.

Father lived for the 'mention,' which meant that the world at large had heard from him once again. Planting his 'mentions' was a Gotham industry.

There was an air of expectation in the room as palpable as an electric current. It was Sunday evening in the fall of 1944 and Phyllis and I were 18. We had graduated from boarding school and in a few weeks would be freshmen at Vassar College. Meanwhile, we were living with our parents in their two-bedroom apartment in Manhattan.

On this night, Phyllis and I and our parents were seated at the dinner table in the sleek compact apartment. It was a small room with beige walls and carpet. A Pissarro painting hung on the wall facing the kitchen, depicting a park scene.

Daddy had told us that there would be a "mention" on Jack Benny's popular radio show that aired at seven. This was not the first time the comedian had delivered an Arthur Murray gag, but I felt as if each of us was holding our breath.

It was now 6:50. Daddy turned on the radio to the CBS station and fiddled with the dial until he was satisfied with the sound.

Finally Don Wilson's rich baritone boomed, "*The Jack Benny Program* presented by America's largest selling cigarette, Lucky Strike." The babble of the tobacco auctioneer. *Lucky Strike Means Fine Tobacco LSMFT*. Strains of "I'm a Yankee Doodle Dandy" segued into Jack's theme song, "Love in Bloom," and Dennis Day burst into the room.

Jack: "Don't ever do that again. I was so scared my hair stood up."

Mary: "Stood up? It jumped off and ran back to Max Factor."

More jokes. Another commercial. Still no mention of Arthur Murray.

"I'm getting hungry," my mother said crossly, interrupting the radio show. "Helen," she called, "we'll have our soup."

Living in the spotlight meant that the rest of us lived in his reflected light.

Once our beloved housekeeper when we lived in the suburbs, Helen now lived in a third-floor walk-up on First Avenue. Mother had summoned her to help on one of the infrequent evenings when we four were having dinner at home. An apron tied over her skirt and blouse, her gray hair in a hairnet, Helen was a reassuring reminder that we were once a family living in a white colonial house in Harrison, New York, with a garden and oak trees. At this time of year there would be the smell of burning leaves.

Responding to Mother's request, Helen appeared, clomping into the room in her black oxford shoes, carrying a tray with a single serving of egg drop soup in a gold rimmed china bowl. Helen frowned, her lower lip clamped on the upper in an effort to keep the chicken soup from spilling. She set the bowl on Mother's china plate, then went back to the kitchen for another serving. "I got *every bit of chicken fat*," Helen whispered to my mother who silenced her with a *ssshh* gesture. She served my father and Phyllis and me. We sipped our soup with heavy monogrammed silver spoons, our heads tilted towards the radio.

"Are you sure it's going to be on?" Mother irritably asked my father. He shrugged. A second later, he held up his hand as if stopping traffic. "Helen, come quick!" Mother called. Helen rushed into the dining room in time to hear Jack Benny say to Mary Livingstone, "I learned to dance at Arthur Murray's."

"That's nice, Jack," Mary replied. "When are you going to start dancing with girls?"

Daddy smiled, Mother looked pleased and told Helen she could serve the roast chicken.

Naturally, such a mention on a leading radio show didn't just happen. This particular gag was planted by a budding young comedy writer named Woody Allen. Allen was one of a stable of fledgling press agents who were paid $25 each time they planted an Arthur Murray mention in a Broadway column or, better still, a top-ranking radio show.

My father didn't depend on press agents to keep his name alive. He and my mother frequented the exclusive Stork Club at 53rd Street where Walter Winchell, the famed columnist, held court at Table 50.

Here's Arthur with Jane Wyman in 1937 doing the Lambeth Walk, which originated in England. Jane was later the first wife of Ronald Reagan, who became president.

On a Saturday evening shortly after the Jack Benny incident, Mother and Daddy asked my sister and me to join them for dinner at the Stork Club. The club special was the chicken hamburger. I didn't relish dancing with my father—I felt clumsy and out of practice—but I enjoyed seeing glamorous Brenda Frazier, the debutante who appeared on the cover of *Life* magazine, and the other debutantes cavort under the soft flattering lights.

When the band struck up a syncopated version of the Mills Brothers' "Paper Doll," Daddy stood up and bowed in my direction. I scrambled to my feet. I was relieved they were playing a jitterbug. This lively dance was less exacting than others, and I liked seeing Daddy put on his "surprise" face—his eyebrows shot up and his mouth made an "O" when he led me in a break step.

On our way back from the dance floor, Daddy stopped by Walter Winchell's table and handed a scrawled note to the famed columnist.

"See if you like this joke," my father smiled shyly.

"You're looking well, Arthur," Winchell mumbled and stuffed the paper in his already bulging jacket pocket.

"Doesn't he have enough jokes?" I asked with the adolescent's whine of disapproval on our way back to our table.

"Not at all," my father said. "Columnists always need material." My father was right, of course, but I thought it was beneath him to be peddling jokes.

I once read the book *Winchell* by Neal Gabler, which confirmed my memory of my father's pleasure in publicity. "Press agents liked to tell the story about dance king Arthur Murray who they described as a dour laconic man," Gabler wrote. "They got him into columns by making him the vehicle for their snappy one-liners."

Then the Arthur Murray name struck a dry period. According to Gabler, my father called his press agent, Art Franklin, and complained.

"What happened, Art?" he asked. "Did I lose my sense of humor?"

Daddy loved this fabricated exchange and never tired of repeating it.

I should have been prepared for such foolishness after spending a year in Beverly Hills when Phyllis and I were 12. One morning in December, Daddy opened the *Los Angeles Times* and scanned Hedda Hopper's column. He gave a little chuckle and passed the paper to Phyllis and me. To our horror, we read: "Arthur Murray's twin daughters, puzzled over seeing a Santa Claus at each street corner, asked, 'Daddy, does Santa Claus have puppies?'"

In an anguished chorus, we wailed our embarrassment. What would the kids at school think when they read this?

"I wouldn't worry," Daddy said. "Your friends don't read the newspaper."

We glared at his bald head bent over the stock market page, but he was right. No one at school said a word.

We didn't think our encounters with press agents could get any worse but they did. That year in Hollywood, we met Milton, Daddy's current press agent, and found out how bad it could get. Our parents were about to leave for New York on business and Phyllis and I planned to stay with our ninth grade teacher, Miss Vahn.

"I asked Milton to call you," Daddy said to us before he and mother left for New York. "He'll probably take you out to some nice place."

As avid movie magazine readers, Phyllis and I were familiar with nightclubs in Hollywood and longed to experience one of these celebrity hangouts. When Milton called and made a date to pick us up at eight o'clock that evening, I fervently hoped he was taking us to the Trocadero. Phyllis bet on Ciro's. In anticipation, we put on our full-skirted, taffeta dresses with two stiff crinolines underneath.

At eight, Milton tooted his horn and we ran out to meet him. "What a lovely car," I said, sliding onto the front seat. My layers of net petticoats acted like springs as we drove through Bel Air in Milton's Ford Deluxe Convertible. "There's Errol Flynn's mansion," Milton said, waving a hand at a large pink stucco house. "And here's where Claudette Colbert lives. There's Gary Cooper's place."

After a while Milton didn't point out any more celebrity homes. We had come to a different part of town with small Spanish style houses set close together. Milton pulled up in front of one of the houses shaded by a hibiscus tree.

"Be right back," he said, leaping out of the car. Phyllis and I craned our necks as we watched him ring the doorbell and disappear inside. Milton emerged a few minutes later with a pretty blonde woman carrying a little gray poodle. She was wearing a low-necked dirndl dress with off-the-shoulder bodice.

"Girls, this is Delores," Milton said hurriedly as he held open the car door.

Delores smiled at us. "If you don't mind," she said, waving her hand at the front seat. We looked puzzled, but then comprehending, Phyllis and I scrambled out of the front seat and maneuvered our wide skirts into the back.

Delores handed the dog to Milton and plumped herself down in the front seat. "Here, Lifey," she said, holding out her arms. "Come to Mommy."

We started off.

"How are you, Milt?" she said in a throaty voice, laying her hand on his arm.

"Never better," he said, kissing her cheek. "Umm, you smell good."

"I wonder where we're going?" Phyllis whispered after we had driven fifteen or twenty minutes. I had been looking out the window wondering the same thing. Suddenly I realized we were back in our neighborhood. We sat in silence as we passed the Warner Brothers theater, neon-lit signs, Armstrong and Shroeder, the Brown Derby. He was taking us home.

Milton turned into our street. "Okay, girls, here we are." He held open the car door. "Hope you enjoyed the ride. Give my best to your parents when you talk to them." Milton zoomed off as we walked up the path to Miss Vahn's apartment house.

Why couldn't Daddy have told Milton where to take us? All he cared about was having his name in the paper. Nobody cared what we wanted. I started to talk to Phyllis but I felt too close to tears to risk speaking. The back of my legs felt scratchy from the stiff petticoats.

After a year, we moved back to New York and, until we found an apartment, began living in a series of hotel suites. By this time, my sister and I were 14, and the name Arthur Murray was well-known. A constant outpouring of newspaper and magazine articles reflected whatever craziness my father's press agents could devise. But it was not until television arrived two decades later that the public recognized my father's deadpan expression and bald head.

In the pre-television era, my father had no hesitation about introducing himself to strangers. One day, he returned from his walk in Central Park and cheerfully related a conversation with a woman he had met on a park bench.

"I told her I was Arthur Murray," he said.

"Oh, Daddy, did you have to tell her who you were?" we said, voicing disapproval as forcefully as we dared.

Daddy looked surprised and faintly annoyed.

"I made her day," he said flatly.

An incident occurred many years later that made me aware that my father would go to any lengths to publicize his name. On a visit to Honolulu, where my parents had retired, Phyllis and I noticed a framed clipping from the May 1962 issue of *Esquire* on the door of my father's bedroom closet. Looking closer, I saw that my father, one of several celebrities, was dressed in costume. To my horror, he wore a Nazi Storm Trooper uniform with a red swastika arm band. Cigarette in hand, he mugged a haughty expression.

"How could he do such a thing?" Phyllis and I said to one another. "How could he?"

But neither of us had the nerve to question him.

2
The young Jane Murray

CHAPTER 6

New York bachelor days

Miss Murray, waiting for Mr. Right.

My dream was to be a playwright. But how to follow such a dream? Stand in the playwright unemployment line? So I began in the mail room of Look magazine.

I looked in the mirror in my father's bathroom and gently patted my pompadour. Today I'm going to discuss the apartment with my mother. *Why am I putting it off? Once she agrees I can start moving my things.*

In September of 1948, I was living in my parents' apartment at 820 Park Avenue. The apartment had only two bedrooms. So when Phyllis and I were home, Daddy moved into Mother's bedroom. My father was as fastidious as Mother so we were careful not to finger his thick book of French Impressionist paintings or touch the circular black glossy coffee table in the living room that showed every finger mark.

I disliked the ritual of nodding "Good morning" or "Evening" to the young doorman dressed in gray livery who looked as if he could do something more demanding than open doors. I felt sorry for the elderly elevator man, in matching uniform, clenching and unclenching his white gloved fingers. He kept his eyes focused on the panel of flashing numbers as if these trips up and down required a captain's surveillance.

When I decided to move out of my parents' apartment, I also moved down.

Phyllis and I had graduated from Sarah Lawrence in June. We had begun at Vassar, then an impromptu inspection had altered our college trajectory. In the war years, with no men around, the Vassar girls didn't dress as they had before, neither did they wash their hair quite so religiously. When Daddy visited, he could not have been more appalled if he had found his daughters serving gin in a roadhouse. In his worldview, all women, even undergraduates, must be impeccably turned out at all times. He began a campaign for us to transfer to Sarah Lawrence, a livelier campus only thirty minutes from New York. And so we followed Daddy's lead.

Soon after our graduation, Phyllis became engaged. I spent the summer attending a radio workshop at the University of Wisconsin. This was the golden age of radio drama, and my dream was to become a playwright.

I wasn't sure how to follow this dream, so I applied for an editorial job at *Look* magazine. Soon after, I received a phone call notifying me that I had a job in the reader mail department. The fly in the ointment was the prospect of living at home. So when Glenn, my best friend at college, asked me to share her basement apartment, I accepted gratefully. But first I needed my parents' permission.

I decided to broach the subject one morning after I had finished breakfast in the dining room. I was still in my pajamas and bathrobe. Mother, dressed in what she called her office uniform—a black wool dress, gold necklace, and earrings—was in constant motion. Coming from the kitchen, she clutched a yellow legal pad. Her high-heeled suede pumps tapped a rhythm on the kitchen floor before she rushed by into the living room. I could smell the warm odor of honey cake that Mother had just taken out of the oven.

I waited until she returned to the dining room and was about to ask me my plans for the day. "Mother, you remember Glenn," I blurted. She wants me to share . . ."

Mother sat down on one of the Chippendale chairs. She looked hurt and bewildered at the prospect of my leaving home. "What will people think?" she wailed. "You have a perfectly good home but you want to move twenty blocks away?"

I wasn't used to defying my parents, but I detected this was a battle that could easily be won, and I was right.

"Do as you want, Baby," she sighed, a few minutes later. "I haven't lost a daughter," she quipped to a friend. "I've gained a bedroom."

Despite the prestigious address of our new apartment, which was next door to the Museum of Modern Art, the monthly rent was only $50. While fifty dollars wouldn't pay the rent on a garage today, at the time it was nearly twice my weekly salary at *Look*. Even so, the apartment lacked amenities. Instead of an electric refrigerator, we had an icebox; an iceman brought a chunk of ice every week. The shower head, perched over a rust-stained tub, emitted only a trickle of hot water. Consequently, my morning shower was a time-consuming affair that entailed placing soaped areas of my anatomy in the path of the feeble stream.

Being an Arthur Murray teacher is the best training in the world, Daddy said. So I obediently went to work at the dancing studio. Here I am, teaching a class.

The only two windows in our basement apartment had thick wrought iron bars and looked out on a continuous parade of shoes. Lacking much natural light, the apartment was shrouded in gloom. It appeared even darker when Glenn and her boyfriend, Jack, painted the walls an inky blue. Even the white touches of woodwork and shutters did not brighten the room. The two lamps in the apartment glowed like torches in a coal mine.

The only serious disadvantage to our "flat," as we called it, was having to share our one room. The room itself had ample space for our two beds, a stove, and an ice chest. Glenn was now going steady with Jack and occasionally the two wished to spend the evening at home. In those days, "nice" girls did not "go all the way," but most approved of a bit of necking. On evenings when Glenn and Jack were together, I wanted to get out of the way. That was when I retired to the bathroom, armed with several issues of *The New Yorker*, a box of Ivory Flakes, and my underwear and stockings.

Most evenings, I had dinner with my own serious beau, a young lawyer I'll call Tom. He once told me that his family was related to British nobility, which I figured might account for his resemblance to Prince Philip. We had met at Sarah Lawrence shortly before graduation. Following a weekend at Williams College where Tom attended, he gave me his Phi Beta Kappa key to wear on a chain around my neck. The gold key nestled cool and reassuring between my breasts.

On a typical evening I'd walk from Cowles Publications at 52nd Street and Madison to meet Tom at The Blue Bowl at 48th Street and Park near his law office. One October evening, Tom was already seated at our table studying the early bird specials.

"How did the trial go?" I asked after the waitress took my order for meat loaf. I could tell by the glint in his eyes that he was prepared to launch into a lengthy description. Taking small bites of a Parker roll, I gazed contentedly at Tom. His lean handsome face still had remnants of a deep tan acquired while sailing at his family's summer house on Fishers Island. He wore a lightweight gray suit from Paul Stuart, a small-figured tie—the kind of preppie look I liked.

He leaned forward with the air of a cat that has cornered its prey. "I knew I had him when I . . ."

Hastily, I brought my attention back to the trial he was describing and searched my mind for another question. Squinting through a cloud of cigarette smoke, Tom looked at his watch, then gestured for the waitress to bring the check. He scrutinized each item carefully, then quickly calculated my share of the dinner. (Before we began our regular dinner dates, we had discussed Tom's finances and in an effort to please I agreed it was only sensible to go dutch.) He then took out a small spiral notebook and wrote down what he spent for dinner. Tom said that he knew to the penny his living expenses. I thought uneasily about the chaotic condition of my checkbook, then brightened, thinking, *After we're married, I'll keep better records.*

"I have a big day tomorrow," he said, with a quick kiss on my lips, and we headed for our respective apartments. Walking home on this clear autumn evening

I hummed a song from *Oklahoma* whose refrain began, "Don't throw bouquets at me . . . ." After unlatching the door of my apartment and finding it empty, I peeled off my black leather gloves and crooned to an imaginary audience, "People will say we're in love."

One Saturday a few weeks after I had moved in with Glenn, my mother called and said she and Daddy would love to see my new apartment. She had a housewarming gift. "All very practical items," she said. After a whispered conference with Glenn, I made a date for the following Saturday at four. Then sitting on my bed—we had only one chair at the time—Glenn and I discussed what to serve. We quickly decided on tea for my parents' visit. Glenn said she'd use her mother's good china teacups.

I made a shopping list—my mother's favorite English tea bags and cookies from a nearby pastry shop. We hoped the undependable gas stove would work, at least well enough to boil water. We rarely used it. Instead of fixing breakfast at home we preferred to go to a nearby Schrafft's, part of an upscale chain of thirty-nine restaurants that flourished in New York up until the late 1960s. Here seated in comfortable leather chairs we enjoyed strong fragrant coffee and moist raisin bran muffins served by waitresses wearing crinkly white aprons and caps.

The afternoon of their visit, I put on my navy blue coat dress with gold buttons and my navy blue pumps that didn't pinch too badly as long as I wasn't walking any distance. The linoleum floor was newly mopped, teacups in readiness on the stove. At the dot of four, there was a knock on the door.

"Knock, knock, who's there?" Mother caroled. She walked in, trailing the scent of Arpège, her red coat swinging about her legs. My father, in his gray cashmere coat, carried a tote bag from Hammacher Schlemmer. "I thought you could use a good paring knife," Mother said, unpacking the tote. I was grateful for Glenn's exuberant thank-you's. I had already become stiff and tongue-tied, as I usually did around my parents.

My father looked around the room, taking in the barred windows. "It's . . . very . . . nice," he said in his halting way of talking. I waited for a humorous comment, but he silently folded his coat and placed it carefully at the foot of my bed.

"Let me have your coat, Madame," he said to Mother, who had launched into a lively monologue about the first dinner party she gave as an 18-year-old bride. When she paused after relating the fiasco of the creme de menthe dessert that wouldn't jell, I quickly asked if everyone would like tea. "I'd love it," Mother answered. My father murmured consent. "I want to see your kitchen," Mother said gaily, and in a moment we four were grouped around the rust-spotted stove.

I filled the kettle with water, and, willing my hands not to shake, lit a match on the jet and turned the switch. To my relief, blue-white flames sprang up. When the water boiled, I removed the kettle and turned off the jet. I was about to fill the teacups when, to my horror, an army of roaches marched out of the jet. Exhibiting the resilience of typical New Yorkers, they continued to move, still in unison, down the side of the stove and mysteriously disappeared.

"You need a good cleaning woman," my father said, first to break the silence.

Glenn appeared undismayed by the incident and, with a charming eye-crinkling smile, described her miserable housekeeping at home. "There were inches of dust in my room. I never hung anything up."

Daddy was in the one chair; we three perched awkwardly on our beds. "How did you know my favorite brand of tea?" Mother beamed at me. My father left his tea untouched and uncharacteristically shook his head at the butter cookies. He glanced uncomfortably at the stove, as if watching for the roaches to reappear.

A few minutes later he put on his coat and held out Mother's coat for her. "Must we leave so soon?" she said imploringly, but he looked unyielding. "We had roaches once in the Harrison house," she said in a comforting tone, buttoning her coat. "They come in on grocery bags."

One Sunday morning in January, I awakened and looked over at Glenn who was in her flannel nightgown propped up on one elbow, admiring her own left hand. Catching sight of my barely opened eyes, Glenn rushed over with a whoop and plopped on my bed. In a rush of words, she disclosed that Jack, the night before, had asked her to marry him.

"He was so cute. He hid the jewelry box behind his back and made me guess." She held out her hand. "Isn't it beautiful? We're planning a June wedding, but I'm going to spend a few months at home getting ready."

I tried to share Glenn's happiness but I was feeling close to tears. With Glenn getting married I'd have to move back home. I groaned inwardly, recalling the humiliating incident that occurred at Christmas just a month earlier.

It was 11 o'clock on Christmas Eve. Glenn was spending the holidays at her parents' house in Greenwich, so I moved back to my parents' apartment for a few days. Tom and I had seen a movie and he was taking me home. I rang the doorbell. Tom carried a tin of Christmas cookies. When we walked into the living room my father greeted us cordially. He wore his beige cashmere bathrobe, his lap covered with dozens of Christmas cards.

"Mother has gone to bed," he said. "Sit down." He opened the tin of cookies and, putting on his reading glasses, peered at them. "They're very nice." He turned to me. "What did Tom get you for Christmas?"

All girlish, I showed off the gold locket inscribed "To Jane from Tom, Xmas 1948" that hung on a chain around my neck. My father turned to Tom. "I should think by this time you'd be giving her a ring."

The hot blush started on my neck, crept up to my face, and spread to my ear lobes. The lights in the room seemed to flicker. Tom mumbled a noncommital reply. He left soon after.

I turned to my father, trying to keep my voice steady. "Daddy, that was so embarrassing." My father looked pensive and wet his lips, a mannerism that generally preceded a lecture. "How long have you been going out with Tom?"

I said, in a barely audible voice, "We met last spring."

He frowned. "You're wasting your time." He folded the bathrobe over his pajama leg. "Either a relationship is going somewhere or it's a dead end."

Later in bed, I dug my nails in my palms and stifled angry tears in my pillow. The worst part was, I knew my father was right.

After Glenn married Jack, I found a new roommate, Marion, a stocky girl from Long Island with a marbles-in-the-mouth accent. Marion invited me to share her apartment on Christopher Street in Greenwich Village. This time I had the luxury of two rooms but there was one shortcoming; even though our apartment was a fourth floor walk-up, we could still feel the subway rumbling beneath us.

One day, to my delight, my grandfather Abe called and said he'd like to visit my new place while he was in the neighborhood. I promptly invited him to dinner. Grampe was a wiry "gent," to use one of his expressions, given to one-liners that he had learned during his stint in vaudeville.

I was secretly pleased that Nana couldn't join us. Although I felt sorry for my grandmother, who had been raised in an orphan asylum, I was annoyed at her for bringing her dog, Sonny, everywhere. He was an ill-tempered Pekinese who kept up a constant yipping.

What should I fix for dinner? My mainstay—the only dish I had ever prepared— was pork chops baked in sour cream, one of the selections from *Casserole Cookery* that "allowed the hostess to enjoy her guests." But on this occasion, I wanted something more challenging. Grampe loved good food. He had introduced me to raw oysters at Cavanaugh's, a Manhattan pub.

"Don't bother with that red stuff," he told me. "Just a squirt of lemon will bring out the flavor."

I thumbed through *The Joy of Cooking* and came upon "sauerbraten." It was a perfect choice for a winter night. Grampe, who had Austrian ancestors, would undoubtedly welcome having one of his native dishes. I assembled the ingredients— vinegar, onion, bay leaves, peppercorns—heated the marinade, and poured it over the meat as Mrs. Rombauer's book directed. The recipe said "marinate the meat for a week or ten days." Regrettably, that was impossible as Grampe's visit was two days away.

As it turned out, the abbreviated marinating time was fortunate because I had failed to notice that Mrs. Rombauer said to refrigerate the meat. On the appointed evening, when my grandfather, considerably winded from the four-flight climb, walked through the door, he was greeted by a smell as pungent as a Second Avenue delicatessen. Grampe ate with gusto and apparently suffered no ill effects.

Living in the Village I enjoyed my new-found independence but was bored with my job in the reader mail department at *Look*. There, in a high-ceilinged room like an old-fashioned classroom, Toni and Janet, also college grads, and I, arranged envelopes. The envelopes were stacked in shoe boxes under the watchful eye of Mrs. Barker, a stocky, no-nonsense woman who wore a housedress to work. Her blunt fingers, busy with envelopes, seemed to have a life of their own.

By mid-afternoon, I was mesmerized watching the hands of the schoolhouse clock pause at each number before jerking ahead to the next.

Mercifully, after six months, I was promoted to the reader correspondent division. I sat at a small desk in a room with a half dozen other correspondents. Each of us had a stack of letters and a dictaphone. I started my day rifling through the letters, most of them handwritten messages on lined paper, deciding which ones to answer first. Then I turned on my dictaphone and, with an air of importance, picked up my hand mike. "Dear Mrs. Smith: Thank you so much for your interesting comments about animal vivisection . . . ."

Although my prep school prophecies had destined me to write for *The New Yorker*, I was quite content talking into my dictaphone each day. I knew that I was just marking time until Mr. Right came along. But where was he? I was 24, long past the magic age of 22 when every girl's dream was to wear an engagement ring at college graduation. I carefully read the engagement notices in *The New York Times*, as if to ferret out the secrets of the girls whose angelic faces appeared there.

Now that Tom and I had broken up, I often fixed a simple supper, generally Campbell's tomato soup and tuna salad. The horns of the taxis on the darkening streets below were a reminder that women in black dresses and furs were speeding to elegant dinner parties with their handsome escorts.

While I was wondering when my hero would appear, unbeknownst to me, two powerful women were acting as matchmakers. One was Mary Dillon, a petite blue-eyed lady whose soft-spoken presence belied her achievements. Mary was chairman of the board of the Brooklyn Union Gas Company, the first woman to hold that position, and at the same time served as president of the board of education. Mary took a dancing lesson every Monday at five, after which she and my parents had dinner at Schrafft's, across the street from the Arthur Murray studio.

For my family, dining at Schrafft's with its comfortable dark wood interior and pretty Irish hostesses who greeted us so warmly, felt like home. Even dinner selections—chicken a la King, roast lamb with mint jelly—reminded me of dishes that Helen used to fix.

The other woman who played a crucial part in my life was a friend of Mary's whom I later met. She was Constance Carraway Yeatman, a published poet from a prominent Tennessee family. Connie fit to perfection the image of the Southern belle though her honeyed accent belied a will of iron.

The plot began when Connie's husband, Dick, fell out of a window. Some months earlier, the slight and obedient Southern gentleman, while washing the window of their Fifth Avenue apartment, had fallen four stories and was taken to the emergency room at Bellevue Hospital. Three days later, he had stopped breathing. A nurse then asked the resident physician, Dr. Henry Heimlich, to pronounce him dead. The young doctor took his pulse and detected a faint beat. He realized that the patient's broken jaw and other facial injuries interfered with his breathing. Dr. Heimlich quickly performed a tracheotomy, inserting a tube through his neck into his windpipe. The patient immediately started breathing through the tube.

During Dick Yeatman's gradual recovery, Hank became well acquainted with Dick's wife, Connie, and her friend Mary Dillon. Mary, who had known our family for many years, was certain that Dr. Heimlich was a perfect match for Kathryn and Arthur's daughter. Nine months after the accident, when Dick was discharged from Bellevue Hospital, the two matchmakers swung into action.

Connie executed the opening move. She invited me to her apartment to read some of her newly published poems. It was a charming scene worthy of Jane Austen: the pretty round-cheeked matron bestowing a smile on the shy ingenue sipping tea.

As if on impulse, Connie put down her book and reached for the telephone. "I'm going to call our darlin' doctor. I know he'd love to meet you."

Within minutes, Dr. Heimlich was on the phone and politely offered to call for me later that evening.

In those days, medical residents were not paid. When inveigled into a blind date by the wife of one of his patients, the resident chose the least expensive option. Dr. Heimlich called for me at nine o'clock and took me to Howard Johnson's ice cream parlor, then at Park Avenue and 59th Street.

Seated in a booth across from him, I studied his craggy good looks. The bushy eyebrows, a hawk-like nose, and firm chin complemented his lean six-foot frame. While he worked his way through two scoops of butter pecan ice cream, savoring each spoonful as if he wanted it to last forever, I plied him with questions. I knew he had been in China during the war.

"What was China like?"

"Interesting."

He took another spoonful.

I plowed on. "Did you always want to be a doctor?"

"I guess so."

Years later, it came as no surprise when the man who became my husband admitted that he was uncomfortable talking one-on-one.

When I asked him about his work, I hit pay dirt. It turned out that his medical passion was the esophagus, which I soon learned was the tube that carries food from the throat to the stomach. A patient whose esophagus had been destroyed or removed had to be fed through a stomach tube, a miserable existence. The operation he had devised would create a new esophagus in these patients. He sketched the operation on a paper napkin.

"You bring the lower part of the stomach upward into the chest . . ."

I listened, entranced, to his medical talk. It was immensely satisfying to hear him describe his life-saving operation. What a welcome change from my parents' conversations about the latest radio comedian or columnist to relate an Arthur Murray joke.

Then I stopped asking questions. Instead, I noticed the birthmark, like a dab of red paint, on his right cheek. I thought about how it would feel to be enfolded in his arms.

When we married after a short courtship, I was delighted to shed my celebrity maiden name for one of an anonymous doctor. Surely, the name "Heimlich" was not likely to appear outside of a medical journal. I felt secure in knowing that I would at last be an ordinary person.

But the fates had something else in mind for me.

CHAPTER 7

The happy housewife

Jane and husband Hank, a natural dancer.

In the 1950s, the

happy housewife

syndrome still held sway

in America. My

thoughts of a writing

life were set aside.

But not for long..

I don't know what could have gone wrong. I followed the recipe very carefully. *Select a piece of veal breast and have the butcher make an opening on the underside.* We sat at the dinette table in our New York apartment. Hank unfolded his napkin. "Something new?" he asked.

"I found this recipe in *McCall's*," I answered. *If it turns out well,* I thought, *I'll have a signature dish to prepare for parties. Everyone will say, 'Jane, this is divine. Will you share the recipe?'*

I watched him put a forkful of veal in his mouth and begin to chew. He looked thoughtful and took another bite.

"How is it?" I asked anxiously. He went on chewing. "Well?"

"Honey, I'm not a good one to judge a fancy dish."

"But does it taste good?"

He hesitated. "I think you could go a little easy on the vinegar."

I took a bite. He was right. The carefully concocted sauce tasted sour, almost burnt.

Later, in bed, I thought of the time I spent preparing the veal dish—the sink full of dishes, my back aching from standing so long. Mother kept calling about the wedding gifts I hadn't acknowledged. "No, Mother, I haven't forgotten." I started to cry, pressing my face in the pillow. Hank enveloped me in his arms. "Honey, you know I didn't marry you for your cooking."

I was not alone in my efforts to produce gourmet meals. Most of the women I knew pored over cookbooks, tried new recipes, and seemed so happy. Janet, who lived across the street, entertained all the time and didn't have any help.

Wasn't housework a career, too? Were the two things always mutually exclusive?

The Happy Housewife Syndrome was rampant in the wake of World War II. Soldiers were home. Rosie the Riveter had exchanged her factory uniform for an apron. Dior's New Look, emphaszing a woman's femininity, ushered in net petticoats, full skirts, the fitted jacket with a nipped in waist. Ad agency copy writers found new ways of expressing the bliss that comes from having a polished floor.

Not all of us fit into this picture of the pretty homemaker vacuuming in high-heeled pumps and a straight skirt. Anyone who knew me as a student at Sarah Lawrence in the late 1940s, would agree that I was ill-suited to be an accomplished homemaker. The girls in my dorm, including my sister, had decorated their rooms with flowered Bates bedspreads, matching curtains and pillows. I preferred the minimalist look. My room was equipped with the bare necessities—a bed, blanket and sheets, a wooden desk, chair, and reading lamp. The only concession to adornment was the cover of a concert program tacked to the wall over my bed. This cover showed the egg-shaped head of Igor Stravinsky. I felt I was making some kind of statement, exhibiting a photo of the unconventional Russian composer.

Perfectly satisfied with my bare room, it wasn't until I had a blind date with a senior from Williams College that I had a change of heart. He invited me to Sunday brunch and asked if he could pick me up in my room.

Moments later, I felt a surge of panic. Girls were expected to decorate their rooms like their mothers decorated their own home. What would my date think of Stravinsky on my bare wall?

A few minutes later, I burst into Phyllis's room. "You've got to help me." After much coaxing, Phyllis sighed and agreed to strip her room of bedspread, pillows and curtains, and lend them to me. She gave another exasperated sigh. "I told you to fix up your room. No, don't try to hang the curtains—you'll make a mess of it."

The next morning my date arrived on the dot. "Nice place," he said, sinking into an arm chair with a cheerful floral design. A few minutes later Marian, whose room was a few doors down, came barging in.

"What in the devil—oh, sorry." She gave a manic laugh and fled. After my date left and Phyllis had collected her furnishings, my room looked cold and uninviting. Later that day, I asked Phyllis if she'd help me decorate.

The idea of fussing with my room was at odds with my bookish self. I had always wanted to be a writer. At graduation from prep school in 1944, I was awarded the coveted Shipley English prize. My stories appeared in the literary magazine, *The Compass*. I was editor of the yearbook. My favorite fantasy was being Jo in *Little Women*. I imagined myself scribbling away in the attic writing fanciful tales that I sold to *The New Yorker*.

For an aspiring writer, Sarah Lawrence was an excellent choice. For much of its history, this former womens' college excelled in preparing its students for their professional roles. Alumnae who benefitted from this approach included Barbara Walters, class of 1953.

My "don," as we called our faculty advisor, was Hortense Fletcher King, playwright, poet, and author, whose soft voice reflected her Louisville, Kentucky, roots. One day during a don conference, I blurted that as the daughter of well-known dancers, I was misplaced.

"I'm not the kind of daughter they wanted—I'm shy, I'm not a good dancer." Ms. Fletcher gave me a smile of indescribable sweetness. "You have rhythm in your writing," she said.

In addition to my college professors, my teachers included prominent writers and dramatists who were working in New York. I signed up for a course in radio drama from Perry Lafferty, who later became senior vice president at NBC. He taught me how to write dialogue. The following year, Richard Parke, then a writer at *The New York Times*, coached me on writing good leads.

These gifted professionals all encouraged me. Mr. Parke told me that I had a gift for feature stories. Mr. Lafferty praised my radio fantasy about a bear who worked as a bank teller. He offered to help me sharpen the piece. Ms. Fletcher told me I was destined to have a promising career as a writer. I was elated with these positive reactions but after graduation made no effort to use these well-placed contacts to help me carve out a career.

The truth seems to be that I fell under the thrall that held so many women in those days, when our images were unwittingly shaped by the romantic notions found in movies and the popular culture. Nancy, a senior and a member of New York society, whose cashmere sweaters came from Bermuda, wore an engagement ring. Her ring finger seemed to be weighted down with an enormous square-cut stone that I felt sure was a valuable ice blue diamond. The diamond caught the light from the windows and occasionally she turned her ring with the index finger and thumb of her right hand. I thought of the cold cream advertisement. *She's lovely, she's engaged, she uses Pond's.* I wondered if I would ever wear a blazing diamond on my left hand.

Where did these notions come from? They may not have been our notions at all, rather a kind of airborne virus, infecting all of us. But soon I would be 25, spinsterhood's jumping off point. One month short of that fateful day, I met Henry Heimlich, a handsome surgeon. What followed was a storybook romance. We were giddy with love, our parents approved, although my in-laws, who had strong ties to the Isaac Wise Synagogue, later confessed that they had qualms about their son marrying a girl with the non-Jewish name of Murray. Soon after, they learned that my father had changed his name from Moses Teichmann and their concerns were put to rest.

When Hank and I met, I was living at my parents' apartment at 820 Park Avenue. Before our wedding, Hank and I searched for our first home. I read the classified "apartments for rent" in *The New York Times* and with my Parker pen neatly copied into a spiral notebook what appeared to be possibilities. I knew just what I wanted—

a brownstone apartment reminiscent of Edith Wharton's turn-of-the-century New York. I could imagine the clip-clop of horses' hooves in the early morning. In the spring, I'd hang plants on the stairway and chat with the newly married young woman next door.

My father had other ideas. While I was making lists and waiting for Hank to go apartment hunting with me, my father wasted no time in finding an apartment

I am the happy bride starting off on our honeymoon in Bermuda. I could never have guessed that we would one day celebrate our 58th anniversary.

that suited *his* needs. He wanted one close enough to where he and Mother lived so he could be assured that I would visit her regularly.

"I've found an apartment for you," my father announced one evening at one of our family dinners at Schrafft's. I looked beseechingly at Hank but my father was already explaining to him that it would be a good investment. "I can buy it for you and when you sell it, you can give me the resale price."

The next day my father secured a key from the doorman and we toured the apartment. On the ground floor of the new brick building was a Gristedes grocery store, an upscale market, and around the corner, a Viennese pastry shop. I thought the exterior looked raw and commercial. We took the elevator to the ninth floor. Opening the apartment door, we stepped into a large living room with an oversized window. The light was so bright I felt as if I needed sunglasses. I couldn't imagine finding a cozy writing nook in this room.

Below the window, taxi horns blared and a bus groaned as it pulled away from the curb.

"It's handsome, Arthur," Mother said reverently, then disappeared into the kitchen. "Come and look, a built-in oven!"

For what seemed an interminable time, we opened closet doors and peered out windows. My father pointed out the generous size of the rooms. It was a well-built apartment that could only grow in value, he said. Finally, we took the elevator down and the doorman hailed a taxi.

"How did you find this?" Mother said, squeezing her husband's arm.

Daddy shrugged. "I was driving by in a cab," he said.

"What do you think, honey?" Hank said. "I know you wanted a brownstone."

"A brownstone!" my father erupted. "That is the greatest hoax. Most of them are in deplorable condition. They get high prices because people think they're romantic."

TO MR. AND MRS. ARTHUR MURRAY

Dear Katie and Arthur:

May 23, 1951

Your announcement that your daughter Jane is marrying an obscure quack named Heimlich on June 3rd saddened me considerably. I've had my eye on Jane for a long time and always hoped that some day you would wind up as my in-laws. Well, she made her choice—one that, I believe, she will ultimately regret. With me, each day would have been 24 hours of gaiety and laughter; with Heimlich she will have a life of viruses, vaccines, surgical instruments and rubber gloves. Only time can decide whether she made the right decision.

Even though I am a bitter, disappointed and disillusioned man I send them both my heartiest congratulations.

Best,
Groucho

P.S. Note to Jane: See that all his nurses are ugly.

The taxi pulled up at the dancing studio. "We'll talk more," my mother said, gathering her purse and gloves. My throat was too tight to reply.

We were so eager to be married that we left major decisions to my parents.

This note shows that Groucho didn't need a cigar and a mustache to get laughs. He was as funny in real life as he was on stage.

I never voiced my objections to the apartment. I felt defeated from the beginning, as if it were all out of my hands. Later, Mother suggested that we work with her decorator, Mr. Wisner. "You like him, don't you?" she said. Mr. Wisner, unsmiling, dressed like an Edwardian gentleman, posed with his umbrella as if it were a walking stick. He chose an orange nubby fabric for two full-size couches. Again, I dumbly agreed, even though I detested orange. With the summer sun pouring in, the couches seemed to generate heat.

Our wedding was a lavish affair that took place in the Persian Room at the Plaza. On ordinary nights, the "Incomparable Hildegarde" and other celebrated performers appeared in the sleek nightclub. The evening of our wedding, the dance floor was a blur of high-heeled ankle-strap sandals and men's glossy black patent shoes. These belonged to the branch managers who had founded Arthur Murray dancing studios throughout the country and abroad. I only knew a few of the managers and had little interest in my own wedding, which resembled an Arthur Murray convention.

Returning to New York after a three-week honeymoon in Bermuda, we discovered that we didn't have the key to our new apartment. "Let's call my parents," Hank suggested. "We can stay with them." I readily agreed. I was comfortable around my in-laws. Pop, as we called Hank's father, was a prison social worker. He was much loved and respected by the prison inmates. Mary, Hank's mother, reminded me of homey Ma Perkins in the radio soap opera, solving everyone's problems. Best of all, my in-laws appeared to approve of everything I did.

Hank's parents were all smiles despite the late hour. Mary scurried for bedding and returned with a well-worn quilt. "Have you called your parents?" Mary prompted us. With a twinge of apprehension, I picked up the phone. My mother answered, her voice trembling with anger when she learned we were spending the night with Mary and Pop. "We would have liked to have been the first to hear about your trip," she said.

I felt so continental wearing my first bikini on a trip to a Greek island. Like most vacations, this one followed a medical meeting.

My father got on the phone. "Your mother has been waiting all evening to hear from you. I should think you'd show more consideration."

"I'm sorry," I said, but he had already hung up. "Damn it," I sobbed and threw my eyeglasses across the room. Hank was astonished. It was his first glimpse into his real in-laws. They were exceedingly generous but their generosity clearly had strings attached. In this case, my parents had paid for our honeymoon and expected some deference.

Hank's day as a surgeon started promptly at 8, so at 6:30 I was in the kitchen in my pale blue Christian Dior peignoir, mules, blusher on my cheeks, my hair fluffed up. At Hank's place at the table was half a grapefruit, neatly sectioned, a grapefruit spoon alongside it. Dressed in a business suit, he ate his grapefruit while I drained crisp bacon on a paper towel and beat two eggs. I took pride in fortifying my husband with a substantial breakfast; chest cases, such as removing portions of the lung for cancer or tuberculosis, often ran as long as six hours, leaving Hank little time for meals.

My new husband looked at his watch. "Honey, I'd better leave." He gave me a tender kiss, then he walked to the elevator and blew me another kiss. I stood at the door and waved to him once more before he disappeared into the elevator.

I mused over how to spend my morning. My mother had made a date with her decorator for the following day, so I thought this would be a good day to clean the bathroom. Breakfast dishes washed, I gathered pail, mop, Ivory flakes. I had cleaned bathtubs but never a whole bathroom, so to make sure the white tiled floor was spotless I poured a generous amount of Ivory flakes into the pail, added hot water from the tub faucet, and poured the sudsy water on the floor. I backed up as if I were on the beach escaping an oncoming wave. Too late. My slippers were soaked.

I added more rinse water but the suds continued to rise. The edge of the beige rug in the bedroom was beginning to darken. I gave a bitter laugh, which turned into a sob. Finally, in a panic, I gathered all the towels in the bathroom and threw them on the floor to staunch the flood.

All through the cleaning fiasco, the intercom kept buzzing. I knew what that meant—it was another babke, the sweet yeast cake my father liked. Ever since I mentioned to my father that Hank was putting on a little weight, he had regularly sent it, or something equally rich, from the Viennese bakery downstairs. I scurried for change for the doorman, then opened the door. He handed me the white box. Carrying the box into the kitchen, I held it for a few seconds over the garbage pail, then angrily shoved it in the refrigerator.

The next day, I studied the recipes in *The Joy of Cooking*. Chicken breasts sounded good but they could be so dry. Maybe lamb shanks would be something different. No, they had to be marinated overnight. Finally, deciding on Chicken Supreme Papillote, I assembled my shopping list and prepared to shop at Gristedes. I changed to my good gray suit since it was important to look my best; I felt ill at ease with knowledgeable wives who squeezed pears for ripeness and confidentially asked for a shoulder of lamb.

Arriving at the store, I paused at the produce department where Joe, with thinning gray hair, was stacking the melons. I held up a cantaloupe. "Joe, will this be ripe by tonight?" Joe frowned, pressed the melon, sniffed it.

"What time are you having dinner?" he said.

"Oh, we usually eat about seven." I stopped, aware that I was being teased. A blush spread over my face as I escaped to the bread and rolls department.

Despite my ineptitude at homemaking, I continued to try to live up to what was called "the Happy Housewife." But it wasn't until I read Betty Friedan's 1963 landmark book, *The Feminine Mystique*, that I began to understand why I felt so out of place. This was the postwar era, Friedan wrote, during which the tastemakers glorified the happy housewife. But, she wrote, "We can no longer ignore that voice within women that says, 'I want something more than my husband and my children and my home."

Yet my own role-playing continued in earnest when, after two years of marriage, we moved from New York to Rye, a suburb fifty minutes from Manhattan, where we bought a ranch house.

I cherished the sense of freedom, being miles away from my parents, and over the next decade, I was a stay-at-home mom with our two boys, born only fifteen months apart. At social gatherings, women asked one another, "How many do *you* have?"

During the eight years in which I failed to conceive another child, I answered apologetically, "Just two."

My fantasy was to be a *Cheaper by the Dozen* mother driving a station wagon full of children to Little League games and piano lessons. This fantasy was shared by countless women, but it was decidedly out of character for me. I was not a born mother. I had never been around babies before our first, Philip, was born. Hank had to show me how to hold our newborn. Fortunately, I decided to nurse my baby, an unfashionable practice at the time, which led to a growing confidence in my mothering abilities.

For a brief time—three months was considered ample for breast feeding— I inhabited a timeless pink world that smelled of Johnson's baby powder. The only sound I was conscious of was my baby's contented sucking and an occasional sigh or quiver.

It didn't matter that the orange couches were hideous and I couldn't make good gravy or decorate a room. I was a mother who sustained her baby's life and no one else could do the job I was doing quite as well.

The relaxed mode of mother and baby soon gave way to two lively little boys who chased each other around our one-story house. At night, I fell into bed, exhausted. A writing career seemed more remote than ever. The fantasy remained what it was—a fantasy.

Inexplicably, after the birth of our second child, I stopped menstruating. Some months later, Hank made an appointment for me to see the chief of endocrinology at New York Hospital. After taking a brief history, this man in a white coat, his face devoid of any expression, prescribed weekly hormone injections. I don't know what was in those injections—I never dreamed of questioning the doctor—but night after night I roamed, sleepless, around our house feeling as wired and crazy as if I had downed innumerable cups of coffee.

After hormonal concoctions failed to restore my normal cycle, I finally discontinued the treatment and resigned myself to having no more children. Anyone taking a look at me might have figured out the problem. I was extremely thin, in fact, I had lost weight during my last pregnancy. I had little appetite or energy and subsisted largely on cottage cheese. In retrospect, I feel certain that Mother Nature figured this scrawny creature was ill-equipped to bear another child. Eight years later, when I had gained back some weight and regained my energy, my periods returned. Within the year, I produced healthy twin girls.

Although I had brooded over my inability to have more children, I stopped short of attempting to find fulfillment in flower arranging and needlepoint. I knew myself too well for that. Instead, I resurrected my childhood dream.

CHAPTER 8

Launching myself

Phyllis and Jane, walking in Central Park.

I was then 'Jane Heimlich, of the Hartford Times.' I was the paper's celebrity columnist, eager for a bit of my own.

I stood in the control room at the University of Wisconsin directing my first play, a thinly disguised drama I had written about my father. "Give me more, more," I coaxed from the actor. "I want more feeling," then a gesture to the music director to bring up the music. Softly, my finger at my lips, the music swells up, UP . . .

It was a thrill to write radio drama. I had been struggling to find my own calling. As much as I enjoyed the tingling excitement of playwriting, I rejected this craft when my flamboyant teacher, Lajos Egri, dropped a bombshell. He told our summer school class that it would be twenty years before any of us could gain recognition as a playwright.

This wouldn't do. I wanted quick returns. As the daughter of Kathryn and Arthur Murray, I wanted to make my own mark. It was hard to be in a family where my parents regularly produced books on how to dance and be popular and were constantly in the spotlight. I had little to show for my writing efforts.

To claim my own identity, I began writing a celebrity column for a local newspaper. When my first column, "Around Town with Jane," was published, I gazed with greedy pleasure at my name in print.

Gradually, writing consumed me. My local column led to my writing a celebrity feature for the *Hartford Times*, a venerable 100-plus-year-old daily newspaper. Phone conversations with press agents were a highlight of the job. I hoped that my clipped manner gave the impression that I was in a busy office and not sitting on my bed, fearful my two boys would burst into the room. After one of those phone calls, I wrote with a flourish on my desk calendar, "lunch with Joan Crawford, 12:30, 21 Club." This was my first interview with a major celebrity.

My first celebrity interview was Joan Crawford. She liked show-and-tell.

It was 1962, the year *What Ever Happened to Baby Jane* thrust the 58-year-old star back into the limelight. On this crisp fall day I had allowed close to two hours for my commute from Rye to Grand Central and a taxi to the restaurant. Once there, I stopped in the ladies' room to check my appearance in the gilded mirror. Reflected, I saw a woman dressed in a tailored gray suit and a blouse with a perky bow tie. My brown hair was neatly fixed in a pageboy fastened with a tortoiseshell barrette.

I smiled at my reflection. Could anyone detect that my lower lip was trembling with nervousness?

In the lounge where people waited for their tables, I introduced myself to the captain. "I'm Jane Heimlich from the *Hartford Times*," affecting a casual air, and asked him to let me know when Miss Crawford arrived. I sat in the lounge, breathing in rich smells of steak and cigarettes, grateful for the time to still my rapid heartbeat. I opened a large black purse and took out my notebook, reread the questions typed on the front page and checked my supply of ball point pens.

The captain suddenly materialized in front of me. "Miss Crawford has arrived. Please follow me."

I sprang to my feet and followed him up the stairs to the Tapestry Room. There, seated at the head of the stairs was the legendary movie queen. She wore a vibrant rose-colored suit with matching gloves and off-the-face hat that reminded me of British royalty. She gave a queenly wave to the man ascending the stairs in front of me, then greeted me with a gracious smile.

Over a crabmeat salad, we discussed some of her favorite roles and her leading men. Then with practiced grace, Miss Crawford, born Lucille LeSueur, segued smoothly into the story of her deprived childhood. "I had two possessions, a tiny mirror and a comb. I loved to dance. Once someone broke a bottle on the floor. I was barefoot and stepped on the glass . . ." Her enormous eyes filled with tears.

At some point in the interview, Miss Crawford discovered that I had not seen *Whatever Happened to Baby Jane*. The truth is, I had avoided seeing the film. I had no desire to watch the well-known scene in which the sadistic Bette Davis served a dead mouse on a silver platter to her invalid sister, portrayed by Joan Crawford. Disregarding my excuses, Miss Crawford sprang into action. She asked the maitre d' to bring her a telephone and, after predictable delays, reached the person in charge of films at Columbia Pictures.

"What do you mean you don't have a copy? I'm with a reporter and I want you to send her . . ."

Ultimately defeated, she slammed the phone, took a few sips of water, and regained her composure.

She had another arrow in her quiver. "I'd like you to see my new penthouse." Miss Crawford had recently married Alfred Steele, president of Pepsi Cola, and they had remodeled a condo at 70th Street and Fifth Avenue. Anxious to get home, I demurred. With a new nanny, I was uneasy being away from the two boys all afternoon. Also, I wanted to type my notes while I could still decipher my scribbles.

Miss Crawford had no intention of accepting another refusal. She airily waved a gloved hand, arguing that her penthouse was only a few blocks away.

"Roland," she said to the captain, "tell my chauffeur we're ready."

Minutes later, the sleek black limo we were riding in pulled up at the canopied entrance of the apartment building. Miss Crawford tossed a tight smile to the doorman, then we took the elevator to her apartment. The maid opened the door. I followed Miss Crawford into the parlor, over glossy wood floors that resounded with her footsteps, then up the white carpeted stairs to her spacious dressing room.

A collection of Margaret Keane's paintings of waif-like little girls with enormous sad eyes hung on the white walls. I could picture little Lucille, as she was called then, with her tiny mirror and comb, her only possessions.

On one side of the room was a row of mirrored doors. Miss Crawford opened one door, revealing a rack of floor-length gowns, each covered in plastic. "Here are the hats that I wear with my red velvet," she said, then moved on to the next closet. "Each daytime suit has its own gloves and hats. My dressy suits with jewelry, gloves, and hats. My casual wear." Despite the chilly temperature of the apartment, I felt a dew of perspiration forming on my upper lip.

Finally, we reached the last mirrored door. I weakly voiced my thanks but Miss Crawford was not through with me. "Let me show you how I pack." Out swung an enormous suitcase. By some ingenious overhead device, outfits wrapped in plastic slid into the suitcase. As she launched into the proper way to pack accessories, I mumbled my thanks and headed for the stairs.

"Wait!" she called after me. I stopped, my hand on the banister. She flashed a dazzlingly wide smile. "I want you to have this . . ."

I walked over to receive my gift, which appeared to be an ordinary wooden hanger covered with white cloth.

After I finally escaped from Miss Crawford, I jumped into a taxi to Grand Central, hurrying to get home. I took the escalator to the lower level, clattered down the steps, and rushed through the black metal gates in time to board the 3:50. Once the antiquated train heaved itself into motion, I gazed through dirty train windows at tattered tenements, then dozed for a minute in the yellow light emanating from fly-specked ceiling fixtures. When the train lurched to a stop, I roused myself and reached in my purse for my black notebook. I anxiously read over my scrawled writing. My heart thudded when I couldn't decipher a word.

Driving from the station in Rye, I gripped the wheel, fervently hoping that Philip and Peter, then 5 and 4, had been well cared for in my absence. Our latest nanny, a soft-spoken young Jamaican woman, had only been with us for a month. *Was she as trustworthy as she seemed?*

My watch showed 5:30 by the time I walked in the house. The boys rushed to greet me.

77

"Where have you been?" they demanded. "You promised to come home early." I weakly explained that it took longer than I thought.

Later, at dinner with my parents at a neighborhood restaurant, my father picked up the scent of my guilt. "If you spent as much time on your house and children as you do on your writing," he remarked matter-of-factly, "your children would be better behaved."

I didn't attempt to defend myself. I was sure I wasn't the only writer who felt she was a bad mother. A notable example was Jean Kerr, playwright and humorist, who lived in a nearby suburb. A mutual friend confided that when Kerr was writing she locked herself in her bedroom, heartlessly ignoring the piteous cries of her children pounding on the door.

Was it possible to be a wife, a mother and a writer? This was a question I often asked myself. It is the kind of question less likely to come up with women today. An acquaintance who wrote poetry advised: "You must treat writing like needlepoint. When time permits, you pick it up. When your family needs you, you put it down." Before Hank came home, I would put the plastic cover on my Royal typewriter, stow away a few typewritten pages—my afternoon's work—and hide the carbon paper, as if erasing signs of an illicit encounter.

While I was struggling to balance motherhood and writing, Hank was becoming increasingly fed up with practicing thoracic surgery in the New York area. In the '50s and '60s, before group practice became popular, a surgeon depended on internists and medical doctors to refer cases. Hank was a brilliant surgeon, one of the best-qualified in both general surgery and chest surgery, but he was a dud at schmoozing doctors who might send him patients.

I saw it as my job to be my husband's helpmate, a Loretta Young in a long hostess gown who would charm members of the medical community. Writing would have to take second place, or perhaps even third.

I began to organize what I hoped would be the first of many dinner parties to help my husband's career. Gripping my soft lead pencil, I made innumerable lists on a yellow legal pad. *Polish silver, wash wine glasses, check tablecloths*. I never considered a less formal style of entertaining. This was the mode my mother had taught me.

The day of one party, the caterer, Addie Burrell, plump-cheeked and in her 60s, sat at the kitchen table placidly slicing mushrooms. Wearing a black straw hat and carrying her tote of kitchen tools, she had taken the commuter train from the 125th Street station near her home in Harlem. Despite my long association with Addie, I was constantly in and out of the kitchen, nervously checking on food preparation.

"Addie, did I get enough string beans for sixteen people?"

"You've got a-plenty," Addie said, reassuringly.

A few minutes later, I was back in the kitchen. "Do you think we should serve the salad as a first course or after the Cornish hens?" She assured me that either way would be just fine.

Before our guests arrived, I made sure goblets and wine glasses were placed properly. I straightened a wobbly candle and arranged placecards according to the diagram on my legal pad. I had placed the doctor we were wooing, chief of a medical service, on my right.

At dinner, I plied him with questions about his work. The bartender filled and refilled the glasses. Relieved that the party was almost over, I drank too much wine. Suddenly I was aware that I was seeing double. The doctor had two heads. I heard myself saying, "I'm shirprised that an attractive man like you is shtill . . ."

The candles flickered, the room began to spin. I took a few sips of water hoping I wouldn't be sick to my stomach. The guests left soon after dinner. We never heard from the chest specialist. I was surprised how much time these parties consumed, time I could have spent on my writing.

In 1959 an event had occurred that further ate into my writing time. My parents built a house next door to us. Since 1950 my parents had produced and appeared in a prime time television show, *The Arthur Murray Party*. The strain they felt was beginning to show. Their solution was to buy a place that would serve as a weekend retreat, and what better choice than one of the last waterfront properties in Rye— right next door to us.

"It's going to be such fun living so close," Mother said gaily. "When I run out of salad dressing I can borrow some from you."

I listened with a sinking heart, too timid to express my feelings that they were invading our lives. When I told Hank of my parents' upcoming move, he was genuinely pleased. Part of the Heimlich credo was that families should spend lots of time together. During the Depression, less fortunate family members frequently moved in with Hank's parents. Good times or bad, the clan, numbering fifteen or twenty, congregated at the elder Heimlichs every Sunday for baseball and cold cuts.

Within a year, my parents' contemporary house and swimming pool were completed. One Friday afternoon, I saw a black limo gliding up the driveway, signaling their arrival. I waited for Mother's phone call.

"Could you and Hank join us for dinner? I made reservations at that French restaurant you like so much." On subsequent calls, she might say, "Shari Lewis and Jeremy are sailing up tomorrow. I know they'd love to see you."

I chided myself for not appreciating my parents' hospitality, but I still had the sense they were taking over my life. But Hank was happy and that was the main thing.

Other incidents compounded my sense of being invaded. After taking a stroll around the property, my father asked, "Do you ever make your bed?"

I angrily resolved to close the curtains on our picture window. Later, the septic tank that we now shared in common, clogged up.

"Your children are using too much toilet paper!" my father accused.

What my father needed was a daughter with gumption, one who would tell him to "mind your own business!" Alas, I was a hothouse bloom, like those anemic- looking children in oil paintings by Gainsborough. I was afraid to challenge my father on anything.

What rankled most were my father's critical remarks about my writing. His copy of my column was soon covered by a scrawl of comments in red ink.

"Throw away the first paragraph," he said. Or commenting on an interview with Victor Borge: "A puff piece won't bring you any readers." As always, my father was right, but I wanted a loving father, not an editor.

We decided the time had come to move away from New York. I bristled at my parents' intrusion. Hank had his own frustrations. Hospital politics were demoralizing. Even attending an opera at the "Met," Hank's perennial passion, had lost its luster, owing to a three-hour bumper-to-bumper commute.

Hank put out feelers that he planned to relocate. Soon after, a doctor friend told him that they were looking for a chief of surgery at The Jewish Hospital in Cincinnati. Hank flew out for an interview and fell in love with the Queen City. After a trip to Cincinnati, I was equally charmed. Leaving New York, especially since it meant being 600 miles from my parents' critical eyes, was a huge incentive.

While I grieved over having to give up my hard-won celebrity column, I was also aware that it was difficult to find anything new to say interviewing a celebrity. I knew that Joan Crawford had told those stories about her childhood over and over again. Then I learned that *Writer's Digest*, the freelance writer's bible, was published in Cincinnati. In fact, I was planning to take my precious back issues of the magazine with me. I visualized getting to know editors in person, perhaps an invite to a cheese and wine party.

Life in Cincinnati looked as if it would be smooth sailing. I never expected what would happen next.

Before the Maneuver

Life in Cincinnati

had an idyllic quality.

Or at least it did

before I found

myself once more

with an uneasy

proximity to fame.

Jane and the doctor, quietly at home.

In the spring of 1970, I was standing inside the handsome leaded glass door of our Victorian house in Clifton, a 150-year-old suburb of Cincinnati. We were living in a rented house just minutes from the university, the hospitals, and downtown.

A diminutive figure stood outside and for a crazy second I thought it was my mother. After my parents had built a house next door to us in Rye, Mother frequently dropped by to critique what choices I made. "Baby, were you able to find another set of napkins with the leaf pattern? I don't think a different color would look well." Everything had to be perfect.

When we were newlyweds in Rye, packages from Hammacher Schlemmer piled up, unopened, around the front door. I didn't want my mother's version of the perfect kitchen with the newest type of blender. I wanted to make my own choices.

What annoyed Hank was his mother-in-law calling at an early hour on a weekend. An early riser, she forgot that newlyweds might like to linger in bed. After one such disruptive call, Hank, normally even-tempered, exploded, "I think your mother calls on purpose."

"We're very inbred," said one of the natives. "We don't often take in newcomers."

Happily, Hank's new position as chief of surgery at the Jewish Hospital in Cincinnati allowed us to have our privacy and make our own decisions. Due in large measure to the helpfulness of new women friends in Cincinnati, we found a furnished Victorian to rent from a university professor and his wife. The charming parlor, rarely used as is generally the case, was furnished with a collection of curved wooden chairs and chaises, some admittedly a little shaky. (I can hear my mother's voice, "Why don't you ask one of your friends for the name of a good cabinet maker who can repair this?")

"Don't you miss your own things?" several women asked me. I didn't say so, of course, but I was relieved to be rid of the horrid orange couches that Mother's decorator had chosen. It was good riddance for the bedroom carpet with the edge still water-streaked from the time I attempted to wash the bathroom floor.

Realizing that the figure standing outside was not my mother, I felt a wave of relief and went to open the door. It was my neighbor, Frances, whose husband, Sam, a rabbi, was an esteemed professor at Hebrew Union College. Sam looked more like the Marlboro man in the cigarette ads than my notion of a rabbi. By contrast, Frances was a tiny thing. I could feel her delicate bones when I hugged her. She handed me a bunch of violets, then another hug. I was touched by her gift. It must have taken so long to pick all those violets.

We stood outside chatting for a few minutes. To my right, beyond the circular driveway, a grove of redbud trees grew from a deep crevice. They blazed with color—not really red—but the purple color of red cabbage. "They bloom for such a short time," Frances said.

Hank was as happy as I in Cincinnati. In some ways, we felt like the couple in the Broadway musical *Brigadoon* who had stumbled into a mysterious Scottish village that appeared for a day once every hundred years. In this city with its German roots, we ex-New Yorkers were thrilled with Cincinnati's old world courtesy. At dinner each night, Hank and I swapped can-you-believe-it stories. I related how a motorist took time to lead me to my destination when he discovered I was a newcomer. Hank's story was about a woman at the Bureau of Motor Vehicles who cut through red tape so his workday would not be interrupted.

The summer of 1971 was the last time the Cincinnati opera performed at the Cincinnati Zoo. For more than fifty years, famous opera singers had contended with temperatures in the 90s, as well as screeching and squawking from peacocks and bellows from other zoo animals.

We hike to the top of Mount LeConte, the third highest peak in the Great Smoky Mountains.

This night, the renowned Spanish soprano Montserrat Caballé was singing Gilda in Verdi's *Rigoletto*. Even in the heat, the generous- sized singer was encased in layers of taffeta and velvet. By contrast, I was wearing a bare sun dress and sandals. I could feel the drops of perspiration steadily falling between my breasts as I sipped a beer. This was much more fun than the formality at New York's Metropolitan Opera. There I wore a strapless bra frequently digging into my sides and a stiff crinoline petticoat under my gown. My high heels pinched my toes.

I can't pretend that every aspect of our move to Cincinnati went smoothly; any couple with children knows this would be absolutely impossible. But the kindness of our new friends made a great difference. They steered us in the direction of a girls' school similar to the one Jan and Liz, our twins, had attended in Rye. Helen, our realtor, found a guitar teacher for Peter. Our eldest, Philip, 15, was already enrolled in a New England boarding school when we moved to Cincinnati.

With small-town friendliness, women invited me to lunch, to play tennis at their clubs, to join their book clubs. I felt like an anthropologist making notes on the habits of the natives: Jews and Gentiles mingle in Cincinnati society.

As newcomers, we were surprised and delighted when members of the hospital board invited us to dinner. Before long, I knew by name the bartenders most in demand and recognized the handiwork of the leading party cooks, most often seemingly tireless middle-aged women. When I saw a bartender pass a platter of snug watercress rolls or cheese puffs, I knew that Freida, stocky and smiling, and her sidekick, Ella, dainty with a faint Irish brogue, were preparing delicious treats in the kitchen.

At first I was uneasy when I saw the sparkling Waterford crystal, the satin-like tablecloth, the lush floral centerpieces. Would I be expected to entertain in this fashion? I soon realized that such parties were business expenses and warranted what my dear Helen, our childhood nurse, would call "putting on the dog." When we became better acquainted with some of the board members I quickly found out that hostesses on other nights—like the rest of us—prepared casserole dishes.

Back east, I often felt as if I needed to "cram" for a party—read *The New York Times* to be up on current affairs or the latest best seller. Here, most of the party talk was about Cincinnati happenings. I also didn't have to be concerned about wearing the latest fashion. My party uniform, a floor-length skirt, the material depending on the season, and a pretty blouse or sweater, was quite acceptable.

Unlike parties that I was accustomed to in Westchester County, where the majority of guests were apt to be strangers from other suburban towns, everyone knew one another at these elegant Cincinnati parties. As I discovered when we began reciprocating the board members' hospitality, more than once I made the laughable mistake of introducing siblings to one another. Many of this group were related. Almost all had grown up in Avondale, an area that in the early decades of the century was populated mainly by German Jews. These well-educated and ambitious citizens built large Tudor houses and played an active part in the city's cultural and business affairs.

At one of the first parties, a handsome gray-haired woman said with a faintly amused smile, "We're very inbred. We don't often take in newcomers." As time went on, several other women repeated the assertion. I realized that our newfound popularity largely rested on Hank's position as chief of surgery at The Jewish Hospital, but I was flattered nevertheless. Word had also gotten around that my parents were Kathryn and Arthur Murray. This added a fillip of interest.

Back east, I was accustomed to think that only Daughters of the American Revolution and other pedigreed Gentiles could claim a proud family history. I soon learned that German Jews, who immigrated to Cincinnati between 1820 and 1870, were equally proud of their ancestry. They called themselves the "Forty-Eighters," named after the unsuccessful German revolution of 1848 that induced them to emigrate.

I learned more about these Jews of German descent when Dr. Walter Pritz and his wife, Betty, invited us to their home one Sunday night. After an informal supper of baked beans and franks, our host, rumpled and professorial in a well-worn sweater with a noticeable moth hole, took us into his study. In a twangy, laconic voice, he described a framed letter hanging over his desk. "My great-great-grandfather, Benjamin Pritz, came here in 1848 from Demmelsdorf, a small Bavarian village. He was 18 years old. He had forty-five cents in his pocket. Benjamin worked as a peddler and made enough money to take a wife."

Eventually, Pritz became a wealthy distiller. This rags-to-riches story is typical of the hard-working members of the Jewish community.

After a year getting settled and making new friends, I was ready to get back to writing. Though eager for the demands and satisfactions of newspaper writing, the only opening at the *Cincinnati Post* I was able to find was "Decorating Editor." My friends howled at the thought of my giving advice on a subject I knew nothing about. I accepted the job, though, nervously telling myself that a good writer can write about anything. It worked out fine. I wrote the decorating column for five years, probing homeowners about their own lives and tastes and quoting knowledgeable architects and interior designers.

I had never been so happy. Our children were enrolled in good schools. I had made a niche for myself as a writer. Tooting around the city in my gray Honda Accord, I interviewed homeowners in both the east and west parts of town. What's the difference between the two? According to a young man on the east side, "You can't get a cappuccino on the west side."

Gone were the days when my well-meaning parents had a stranglehold on our lives. Gone was the endless celebrity talk about their appearance on *The Merv Griffin Show* or quips in Walter Winchell's column. Once again, I was grateful that the name "Heimlich" would only appear in a medical journal, not a gossipy *People* magazine.

As the fall season geared up, I felt a growing pride in Cincinnati's cultural treasures. We wasted no time in subscribing to the Cincinnati Symphony, the fifth-oldest orchestra in the United States. Considering the importance of the arts in Cincinnati, it annoyed me when New York friends acted as if we were living in the boondocks. The patronizing response was, "You can always come to New York for the theater." Few were aware at the time that we had an outstanding theater of our own.

The pleasures of Cincinnati went on and on. I was invited to join one of the literary clubs, this one over a hundred years old. I didn't intend to write about decorating much longer, though it had been a good experience. Our children were settled and happy. I had made a few close friends with whom I could let my hair down.

My life now felt as comfortable as a down cushion and as predictable as a road map.

And then the Heimlich Maneuver turned our lives upside down.

Celebrity hoopla

In our Dutch Colonial house, we look like the perfect couple.

Personal matters

were not discussed,

even with close friends.

There was, I soon

learned, no need.

Everyone knew

everything, anyway.

The Heimlich Maneuver had its beginning at our kitchen table one Sunday morning in 1973. Hank was leafing through *The New York Times* when something caught his attention.

"Listen to this: '4,000 people die from food-choking every year in this country. Choking is the sixth leading cause of accidental death.'" He looked surprised. "I didn't think there were so many." I gave a wifely *hmmnn* and went on reading the paper.

Surely, you would expect a doctor's wife to remember how an emergency medical treatment—one of the most important and useful of our time—was devised. Of course, my husband and I discussed the progress of the experiment at dinner. But truthfully, I found that the information about "the endotrachial tube" or "the air flow generated by subdiaphragmatic pressure" went right out of my head.

One thing I remember was that the experiment that led to the Heimlich Maneuver involved three beagle dogs. These dogs were anesthetized to prevent them feeling any pain. And I remember, as if it were a movie, the happy ending to this small-scale experiment. Over a period of weeks, Hank had proven to his satisfaction where on the dog's abdomen to place his fist to prevent choking.

That last day, he asked his assistant to run down to the kitchen and bring him a piece of meat. Hank inserted the meat into the dog's windpipe, pressed on the diaphragm, and the meat flew out of the dog's mouth. "I've found the right treatment for choking," he told me later.

In June of 1974, six months after Hank completed his experiment with the beagle dogs, I was in the kitchen fixing dinner. My husband, beaming, brought home a copy of *Emergency Medicine*. I turned quickly to the article, "Pop Goes the Cafe Coronary." ("Cafe Coronary" refers to the misconception at that time that someone choking on food, which commonly occurred in restaurants, was having a heart attack.) This was the first published report of "subdiaphragmatic pressure," as Hank called his method to save a choking person. Two months later, editors of the *Journal of the American Medical Association* dubbed it "the Heimlich Maneuver."

The article described Hank's method and his dog research, but there were no accounts of people being saved. As yet, no one had tried the method on a choking person. "Now if we can just get the word out to the public," Hank said.

"Wouldn't it be better to wait until you see if it works?" I ventured, ever cautious. Hank gave me a puzzled look.

"I know it will work. It makes perfect sense. Pushing upward on the diaphragm compresses the lungs, which creates a flow of air that moves the object away from the lungs toward the mouth. The lungs act like a bellows." Trying out a new method on the public is nothing new, he explained. "That's how Jonas Salk and Albert Sabin proved that the polio vaccine worked. They inoculated thousands of people—Salk in Indonesia and Sabin in Russia—and then waited for the results. None of the inoculated people developed polio."

Hank's plan to "inoculate" the public with information about his method was set in motion almost immediately. Arthur Snider, a medical reporter on the *Chicago Daily News*, who was familiar with Hank's inventions, wrote a syndicated article describing the choking method. Snider's article appeared in several hundred newspapers all over the country.

Within a few days, the first report of a "save" appeared in the *Seattle Times*. A retired restauranteur named Isaac was at home when a neighbor ran over calling for help. The neighbor's wife, Irene, had collapsed at the dinner table. Isaac had read Snider's article in the *Seattle Times* with special interest, recalling the number of patrons who had choked to death at his restaurant. Rushing next door with his distraught neighbor, the two men found Irene slumped at the table. Isaac performed the method he had just read about. A large piece of chicken flew out of Irene's mouth and she immediately recovered.

During the next few weeks, our mail was flooded with similar accounts that appeared in newspapers all over the country. "Listen to this," Hank said at dinner, reading a clipping from the *Plain Dealer*, "I grabbed her around the waist and a piece of meat hit the opposite wall. And here's another . . . ."

"It's wonderful," I murmured over and over. But I thought to myself, *You sound like Lawrence Welk. 'Won-nerful, won-nerful.'*

Hank put down the clipping he was reading. "Are you listening?"

"Of course," I said, but peevishly thought to myself, *Once in a while couldn't we talk about something else?* During the next few weeks the phone rang constantly. One of the calls was a phone interview with the host of a medical show.

"Keep the kids quiet, please," Hank said, sprawled in his Barcalounger with the phone at his ear. "It's like a bellows," he patiently explained. "The flow of air forces the object out of the mouth." He nodded his head to his unseen caller. "You got it." He made a date to appear on a TV show in Phoenix. "Honey, pick out a tie that goes with the gray plaid sports jacket. That little spot? They'll never notice it. Yeah, I guess I need some new clothes."

The next day, Hank called me from the office. He could barely conceal his excitement. "Honey, guess what? I got a call from the *Today* show. Yeah that's Barbara Walters. They want me on Friday morning. I'll fly to New York Thursday afternoon. They're putting me up at the Essex House."

My mouth went dry, my heart pounded. *Here we go again. The media calling, the TV shows. Celebrity gossip among the guests in the Green Room waiting to go on the show.* I feel as if I'm watching the rerun of a movie about my early life, trying to deal with my parents' fame. The celebrity hoopla gathered steam. The following week I sat on the couch of our living room in Cincinnati waiting for Hank's appearance with Johnny Carson on *The Tonight Show*. I wish I'd let the kids stay up. It had been such a long evening. I was a trifle nervous. I had never seen Johnny Carson—he came on too late for me—but I was familiar with his reputation as a leading comedian.

I needn't have worried. Hank was all smiles and confidence, a hint of dimples, in a European-cut suit. What ever happened to his gray Brooks Brothers? I hadn't noticed before but he was wearing sideburns. He had draped a strand of brown hair over his bald spot.

Hank and Johnny traded quips. Johnny imitated a choking person. Hank reminded him that a choking person cannot speak. Hank flashed a winning smile. "It's the first time you've been silent on the show," he said. The audience roared.

I turned off the TV and got ready for bed. I looked in the bathroom mirror at my troubled face. *Where were we heading?*

Celebrities like to be with other celebrities. As the daughter of a well-known couple and now the wife of a famous doctor, that's one thing I had learned. So it didn't surprise me when Irma Lazarus, a celebrated Cincinnati hostess and tireless patron of the arts, plucked us from our comfortable social life in Clifton and included us in her circle of Beautiful People.

Irma's husband, Fred, a son of the founder of Federated Department Stores, was a fine cook. He was always in the kitchen, pots bubbling, or serving a regional delicacy, often a spicy meat appetizer, to their guests. At a party at their house one sweltering day, I watched Fred stir an enormous pot of spaghetti sauce while their guests frolicked in the swimming pool.

When we first met Irma, her most pressing mission was to find a house for Thomas Schippers, newly-appointed music director of the Cincinnati Symphony Orchestra. Schippers, who had made his debut at New York's Metropolitan Opera at age 23, was as handsome as a Greek god. He had married Elaine Lane "Nonie" Phipps, a willowy beauty, heiress to the Grace shipping fortune. Nonie reminded me of Violetta in *La Traviata*. Only months before her death from lung cancer, she appeared at an opera reception, as gracious as ever in a beautiful evening gown.

Hank and I were also looking for a house; the owners of our beloved Victorian would be returning soon. When Irma learned we were house-hunting, she showed us all the maestro's rejects. One was the four-bedroom 1910 Dutch Colonial located next to Summit School, a Catholic day school. Tommy wanted something much grander, Irma said, but it was perfect for the Heimlich family. We soon got used to the sound of school bells and the cacophony of young voices at recess.

At Irma and Fred's after-symphony parties, we met the musical greats appearing at Music Hall. I could never bring myself to call Leonard Bernstein "Lennie," but Hank had no qualms about familiarity and even played chopsticks with the celebrated performer who was perhaps best known as the composer of the *West Side Story*.

The only celebrity guest whom I felt truly comfortable with was Carol Channing; like my mother, Carol was intent on pleasing others. One evening at Fred and Irma's, I watched with amazement as Carol addressed a half dozen Cincinnati guests by name.

"How do you do it?" I asked. Carol widened her enormous eyes and breathlessly imparted her secret. "I have a lit-tle black book and when the party is over I write down every name."

Hank was spending more and more time with "Tommy" Schippers; the two had a running gag as to which one was more famous. Their laughing over this joke seemed idiotic until it occurred to me that part of the attraction may have been Schippers' beautiful social secretary. She was my opposite—fun-loving, flirtatious, with a mane of blonde hair. In my mind, I labeled her the Golden Girl. In her presence, I felt overly serious, boring, frumpy.

Life became increasingly unreal. Irma and Fred chartered a forty-six-foot sloop and invited us and another couple to sail with them and tour the Greek Islands. The sloop was equipped with a captain and his French wife, who prepared our delicious meals. On board, the conversation was mainly about food. I stretched out on the upper deck enjoying the sun on my back but unable to connect with any of our group. Hank seemed more like a stranger to me, joking with Irma about Tommy and his ménage.

Back in Cincinnati, more invitations came from unexpected sources. A much-married tennis buddy of Hank's, presently between wives, invited us to a cocktail party at his sleek condo. I looked around the room. The women were all young and pretty in tight-fitting black cocktail dresses. One, with a neckline that left nothing to the imagination, was talking to Hank. She put her hand on his arm. I felt my stomach lurch. Driving home, Hank said, "We ought to see more of this crowd."

At an outdoor Labor Day party, I danced a jitterbug with a young gay man. In a bored fashion, he twirled me this way and that, forcing me to strut like a pet monkey. Over my partner's shoulder I saw my husband dancing with the Golden Girl. They were laughing; she wrapped her arm around his neck. She whispered something in his ear, and they left the dance floor.

That winter had a surrealistic quality. The weather was unusually cold, and I imagined there was ice everywhere; it crunched under my feet. I felt as if I were Liv Ullmann in Ingmar Bergman's *Scenes from a Marriage*. Hank and I had been watching this film on television. We sat on opposite ends of the couch, mesmerized by the melancholy story of a relationship as it slowly fell apart.

In real life, I behaved in the most irrational manner. I took pains with my looks, wore pumps in the daytime, and asked my husband if he would like some tea or coffee as if I were a stewardess. ('Flight attendant' had not yet entered the lingo.) If I were gracious enough, attractive enough, my husband would love me.

At the same time, I fantasized about having sex with the professor I was interviewing for my newspaper feature that day. I seriously thought of propositioning the college son of a woman friend to improve my performance in bed. Instead, I sat at my desk and recited a line of poetry that made me think of a gloomy Scottish ballad: *My study has become a widow's walk.*

As every woman who has experienced a rift in her marriage knows, the pain of betrayal is as palpable as physical pain. In my case, the pain served a purpose. Nothing else would have induced me to cut loose the shackles that bound me to the past and begin to become my own person. But the process didn't happen overnight.

I was tempted to dramatize my misery, tell the world how I had sufffered. But in that long, dark tunnel of sleepless nights, I had to admit that I was not the loving wife I had wanted to be. Hank used to joke, half angry, "You sound just like your mother." When I found myself being judgmental, criticizing one of the children or expecting too much of myself, I felt like my father.

Where was the playful creature I had been, brimming with warmth and whimsy? I was still trying to please my father, as my mother had done all her married life. Worse, I was treating my husband with the same deference that I accorded my father. I once saw a movie in which the betrayed wife heaves one plate after another at the errant husband. I longed to do the same, but instead I continued to act as "the pleaser."

How did my father gain his power? I felt that if I understood this complex figure, I could be my own person. Even, perhaps, heave a plate.

3
In search of my father

CHAPTER 11

An immigrant's journey

Arthur's secret weapon was his business sense.

Father was a man of control: his will penetrated into the smallest family crevice. A closer look shed light on what so relentlessly drove him.

My father was the family godfather. All of us feared him and, God forbid, never crossed him. We allowed him to control our lives with the weapon he was as comfortable with as a Japanese samurai fingering the blade of his sword: money.

I watched him manipulate my grandfather Abe, my mother's father. Grampe fit the classic picture of a newspaper man. He loved the daily feat of putting a paper together. He also loved having a couple of drinks with his buddies after work.

When my grandfather reached his mid-60s, my father decided it was time for him to retire. He had many reasons for this; one was that Nana was taking up so much of my mother's time, constantly calling her at the dancing studio and complaining that she was lonesome. My father thought she was a tiresome, self-centered woman and the sooner he got her off Kathryn's back the better.

Delving into the family's dim past, I was surprised at what I found there.

I once witnessed my father nail his prey. This took place on one of my grandparents' Sunday afternoon visits to our Park Avenue apartment. We were all in the living room. My mother was at her desk, paying bills. My grandparents sat at either end of the couch facing my father who was enthroned in his armchair, which was covered in a bold floral pattern.

Between Arthur and his in-laws was a gleaming black circular table that made me think of a nightclub.

My father wasted no time. "Abe, when are you planning to retire?" Grampe shifted his position on the couch, a foolish smile on his face. "I figure I've got a few good years left in me. Nobody's promising me a gold watch." He smiled some more.

"I think you're being very foolish. You had a bad cold last winter . . ." My father, his mouth twitching with impatience, listened to Grampe's lame rejoinder, then delivered the killing blow: "I've bought you and Lenore a condo in St. Petersburg. You'll be near all the shops."

Lenore burst into happy tears and turned to her shell-shocked husband. "Abe, did you hear that?"

Some months later, my grandparents moved to Florida. The next year, Grampe developed stomach cancer and died six months later. At the time, I felt only a dull sense of loss, but, years later, I wondered whether my father's manipulations had hastened Grampe's death.

Over the years, I watched my father manipulate other family members. Deciding that my twin sister, who had been divorced for fifteen years, was getting a bad reputation, he coerced her into marrying a man she did not love. To get his way, he threatened to dissolve her trust fund.

Later, when he and my mother had retired to Honolulu, he induced his granddaughter Martha to move there with her family by creating a job for Martha's husband, Tim. The job, as stockbroker in a prestigious investment firm, turned out to be a disaster for Tim, an artist. But the move accomplished my father's purpose: it gave Kathryn several years in which to live close to her granddaughter.

On more occasions than I care to remember, Hank and I also allowed my father to take control of our lives. His control began when we were a newly engaged couple dizzy with love. My father's opening move was to "give" us the swanky apartment on Madison Avenue, a few blocks from his and mother's home on Park Avenue.

A family portrait of Sara and Abraham Teichman and their five children. Arthur stands next to his mother.

Such splendor left me cold, especially when I realized there would be strings attached. I had been blissfully happy in my series of run-down bachelor apartments where I had lived after college. But like obedient children, Hank and I let my father convince us that it was good business for him to buy the apartment. "It's a tax write-off for me," Daddy said.

As I had dimly anticipated, my father's gift thrust me back into my parents' world, which I had briefly escaped. That grand apartment required the services of an interior designer and a cleaning maid. Gone were the friendly mom-and-pop grocery stores that had been part of my newfound independence. I felt compelled to "dress up" every time I left the apartment and walked by the uniformed doorman who assumed a stiff sentry pose. I missed the easy camaraderie with next-door neighbors. Here, tenants who rode in the elevator studiously avoided eye contact.

Life in the Madison Avenue apartment was an unfortunate beginning for a marriage. My husband and I both knew we had made a grievous mistake accepting my father's gift, but feeling stuck, we even refrained from discussing it with one another.

We fell into the same trap a few years later when we found our house on Long

Island Sound in Rye, New York. While we were figuring out how we could manage mortgage payments, my father quickly stepped in and offered to lend us the money to buy the house.

"It will be a good investment for me," he explained, which it proved to be. But with that gift we lost the last vestige of our independence. Some years later, when my parents proposed building a house next door to us, I felt a sickening lurch in the pit of my stomach but remained silent. By then I felt too indebted to my father to voice the terrible realization that we had lost our independence.

All my life I resented my father controlling all of us. I nursed that resentment until the day he died. Years afterward, I began to think of the way he controlled his family. I began to suspect that the dark chapter of his childhood contained the clues to understanding his enigmatic personality. But I knew little about these early years. My father rarely mentioned his childhood, and I never thought to question him.

My father's parents, Sara and Abraham Teichman, were shadowy figures to me. I knew them only as old people who spoke Yiddish. I had no idea what their life was like in the Old Country, or what impelled them to leave their home and cross the Atlantic. What was it like to live in a tenement on the Lower East Side in the 1890s? What kind of parents were they? Who taught my father to control the lives of others as easily as a puppet master pulls the strings?

With both my parents gone, who was left to answer my questions? I reread my mother's book, *My Husband, Arthur Murray*. It's a lively account of a remarkable man told by his admiring wife. But I looked in vain for insight into these two complex beings. My mother glossed over so much of the pain my father had caused her.

I needed more information than I could find in Mother's book so I turned to my father's brother, Ira. He was the only remaining one of my father's five siblings. I had only brief glimpses of Ira and his gentle and accommodating wife, Ann. I recalled him as a short man, a bantam rooster, cheerful and cocky. Having a head for business like his brother Arthur, Ira went from a successful stint in real estate to a new career as an Arthur Murray branch manager. Then, in the mid-1940s, he, too, like my father before him, changed his name: from Israel Teichman to Ira Murray. Eventually he operated ten flourishing dancing studios in Canada.

In 2002, I calculated that Ira must be in his late 90s. Was he well, his memory and hearing intact? Would he be willing to talk to me? And where did he and Ann live? Feeling a bit uneasy, I called a cousin, Wendy Teichman, with whom I had talked sporadically over the years. Wendy assured me that Ira was alert and well, and she gave me his phone number in Hollywood, Florida.

Still experiencing a slight flutter of nervousness, I called him. I needn't have worried how he'd react to my call. After Ira's initial surprise at hearing from me, he launched into reminiscences. "Arthur and I had a love-hate relationship," he said. "He always fought me but I waited for the right opportunity. I won in the end." That's the tactic I needed in dealing with my father, I thought ruefully—Ira's street-smart feistiness. The hothouse flower I had been raised to be was no match for a man whose personality had been shaped in the cauldron of slum life.

It was Ira's recollections, sounding as fresh as if they had happened yesterday, that led me on a journey back in time. This was a story that began with Arthur's parents, Abraham and Sara, struggling to eke out a livelihood in the *shtetl*, the Yiddish term for a small town. Their town bordered Austria and Poland. I began to realize how tough my grandparents' early life had been. Most Jews lived mainly on bread and potatoes, occasionally herring, a little meat on *Shabbos*. Many were on the verge of starvation. Home was a poorly ventilated, overcrowded wooden hovel with a clay floor and sooty ceiling that dropped filth whenever the oven was lit.

They had little hope of improving their condition. The Austro-Hungarian government prohibited Jews from owning land or traveling freely. They were barred from all government jobs and had to live doing odd jobs, trading with peasants, acting as petty middlemen, tailors, and dairymen.

The Lower East Side: who would have guessed that a shy young man from the slums of New York would inspire millions to dance?

In this world of hostile government officials and empty bellies, religion became the focus of the Jews' lives. Rituals governed all aspects of behavior and diet. I thought of my father ridiculing his father. "All he does is pray," my father said contemptuously. I had fresh sympathy for this small quiet man who was at home in a society where being a scholar was considered the highest calling. Studying Hebrew, the holy language, was the pathway to God.

"Every *shtetl* had its men who did nothing but study the Talmud," Ira said, his voice revealing what he thought of this arrangement. "Women often became breadwinners so husbands could devote themselves to study."

Sara, my father's mother, a tall commanding presence even as an old lady, ranked socially above her husband, Ira explained. "Her father was not only a rabbi but presided as a judge, settling differences among Jews." Abraham was a small, unprepossessing man who worked as a clerk in the granary. Nevertheless, when the *shadkhin*, the matchmaker, proposed a marriage between Sara and Abraham, Sara's father quickly accepted. In the *shtetl* where so many Jews were unemployed, a prospective son-in-law who had a job was considered a good catch. Within two years, the couple produced two children, Rebecca, firstborn, and Moishe, my father.

After they married, the couple leased a tavern from the local baron, who, as an agent of the Czar, controlled the town's revenue. They sold food and whiskey to Polish workers but soon discovered they were not allowed to make a profit. It was bad enough to work for nothing but galling as well to the proud rabbi's daughter, who waited on coarse peasants who spat on the floor. The peasants, in turn, despised this snooty *jüdin* and set the couple's house on fire several times. The third time, Sara feared for her life and told her husband they must leave.

By this time, the 1890s, escape was possible for *shtetl* Jews. Stories circulated about the magic land of America. Letters came from former townspeople who had immigrated to the new world. The letters contained snapshots of a once-destitute tailor or butcher boy now dressed in fancy clothes. Sara prodded her meek husband to go to the baron and ask permission to emigrate. The baron refused, but when Abraham broke down in tears, he relented.

Abraham and Sara had only enough money for one passage. Sara and the two children, Rebecca and 1-year old Moishe, would have to come later. During the next year, Abraham made enough money giving Hebrew lessons and selling paper clips and pencils on street corners to pay for his family's passage. In 1896, Sara joined the exodus of two million Jews, most from eastern Europe, who, starting in the 1880s, and continuing for several decades, emigrated to the United States. One out of every three Jews joined this mass migration. They came because they were hungry and persecuted; life in their homeland had become intolerable.

I tried to imagine what it was like to leave your own village, poor as it was, and travel to an unknown country where you didn't speak the language, you had no friends, and possibly no relatives. It's important to realize that not all the Jews who suffered from hunger or the brutality of pogroms emigrated. Two-thirds stayed. The one-third who had the courage to leave were a special breed; energetic, adventurous, determined to achieve a better life for themselves and their children.

What I learned from Ira about the trip across the Atlantic would give anyone pause. It was an ordeal we can hardly imagine today. Immigrants had to make their way to the ship on foot, or by train, or, most likely, by horse and wagon. After scraping from the last of their savings, few had money for costly passports. They had to bribe officials at border crossings. The worst part lay ahead—the terror of the Atlantic and the miserable conditions imposed upon passengers traveling in steerage.

The trip lasted about sixteen days. Everyone in steerage was herded into a dark filthy compartment that held over three hundred. There was no privacy. A steerage berth was an iron bunk with a straw mattress and no pillow. It was never cleaned. There was no place to store clothes or household possessions. A family's entire belongings had to be piled on the berth.

With hundreds of people packed below decks together and seasick for days, the floor was awash with vomit. Toilets were few and foul smelling. Inedible food was served from huge kettles into dinner pails. The bread often turned moldy; water was scarce. Still ahead, the ordeal of the medical exam at Ellis Island upon arrival in port awaited the immigrants. Abraham no doubt feared that the exam would detect trachoma or tuberculosis, and, after this long ordeal, he could still be deported.

Learning what my grandparents endured made me realize what tough, resilient stock my father came from. One day it occurred to me that if it were not for the courage of my grandparents I might have ended my life in a concentration camp.

But crossing the Atlantic was only one of the early experiences that shaped my father. Ahead lay the teeming slums of the Lower East Side, which proved an apt training ground for the grooming of a godfather.

OUT *of* STEP

An immigrant's journey

103

CHAPTER 12

A Yiddish Machiavelli

Sara Teichman, the rabbi's daughter.

To understand my father, one must first understand how tightly his mother tied the parental knot. She wasn't easily pleased, and neither was he.

I never understood my father until I learned about his mother, Sara Teichman. By any standard, she was cruel and unfeeling. She belittled her five offspring, told them they'd never amount to anything. And yet, in those children who were strong enough to stand up to her, she instilled an unshakable desire to succeed. Under her iron tutelage, my father learned to be tough and demanding, to rule his family as if by divine right. She also taught him to use deceit to achieve his aims, as I discovered in a shocking episode.

For two weeks, on a ship bound for America, Sara and her two children, Rebecca and Moishe, endured the filthy prison-like confines of steerage. They finally arrived at Ellis Island. Abraham met them at the dock. A small, unprepossessing man, he had a few pennies in his pocket to pay for their fare on the horse-drawn street car to the Lower East Side. Ahead stretched several years of bruising poverty until Sara opened a bakery, the first step on the road to prosperity.

Sara Teichman was a tall, handsome woman whose neighbors looked to her for advice. Pushcart dealers knew her as a shrewd shopper who could spot an egg that wasn't fresh or herring past its prime. She knew how to stretch the ends and bones of a *flanken* that the butcher sold for six cents a pound so her family always had meat soup on Friday nights. As a special treat, she made *taiglach*, honey candy or honey cake. Her needle flew as she stitched the boys' cotton shirts. Moishe, the eldest of four brothers, did all the family ironing, which he performed in his accustomed manner—perfectly, just as his mother would have done.

Sara was a rabbi's daughter who had no use for religion. What had it given her?

While the world of pushcarts and slum living seemed far removed from the gracefully decorated white colonial house my parents lived in years later, my father never forgot his upbringing. When I learned that he was the one who did the family ironing, I understood why my father was so fussy about his shirts. One day, when I was 8 or 9, he showed Helen one of his London-made shirts. He instructed her how to avoid a crease in the sleeve. Helen, who prided herself on her domestic skills, glowered at his criticism.

After repeated instances of such fault-finding, Helen announced she was fed up and they better find somebody else who could put up with him. Afterward, Mother, in a desperate effort to restore peace, had a long talk with Helen in the kitchen. We could hear Mother's nervous words of endearment, which she spread like honey. Still, it was several days before Helen lost her mad face.

Shirts were not the only domain my father took over. He also appropriated the entire kitchen. As newlyweds, my mother considered their new kitchen to be spotless until Arthur put on a pair of white cotton gloves and ran his fingers along the top of the tall refrigerator. He held out his gloved hand to his bewildered young wife. Unmistakable evidence.

My mother never stopped trying to please her perfectionist husband. Over the years, she tried one honey cake recipe after another until she produced a buttercup yellow specimen that Arthur pronounced was just like his mother's.

Arthur's mother was much more than a *baleboste*, the boss of the household. Sara had a head for business. A few years after they settled on the Lower East Side, enterprising Sara spied a new building across the street with a basement that she thought would make a good bakery. Like so many immigrants from eastern Europe, she missed the dark, sour, chewy rye bread that was called "corn bread," even though it contained no corn.

Sara had no money to pay for ovens or hire a baker, but because she was known as an honest, hard-working woman, the builder agreed to install them on credit. Thus, in the basement, the oven began to turn out fragrant loaves of bread. Upstairs, she sold different varieties of bread—corn bread, rye bread, challah. Within a year, she had paid back the loan.

As times got better, Sara gave up the bakery and worked with her husband in real estate. Sara was an expert when it came to a closing. No matter that she only spoke and read Yiddish. She was dealing with her own people. She not only knew the nuances of the language but understood the customs these newly arrived immigrants brought with them and their difficulties in adjusting to a new life. She soon earned the reputation of being a shrewd, tough businesswoman.

Sara was equally tough and demanding as a wife. "My mother and father were always fighting," said Ira, my father's youngest brother, describing his parents' loveless marriage. "My mother talked against my father in front of us children." Much of their wrangling centered on religion. "My father was very religious. My mother had given up on God."

Although she was a rabbi's daughter, Sara had no use for religion. What had God ever done for her? When their baby was very sick, the doctor refused to treat a Jewish child. The baby died. She mocked her husband who clung to the religious practices of the *shtetl*. "Where was God when the peasants set fire to our house?" she asked him.

And here in America, there wasn't time to pore over the Talmud, put on a *tallis* (prayer shawl), and mutter prayers twice a day. "We need to eat," she told him. "You can't eat prayers." Abraham, bewildered by the ways of the New World, clung to the religious rituals of the *shtetl*. But despite his pleas, Sara refused to keep a kosher house or light candles on the Sabbath.

She would stop at nothing to achieve her own ends. As Ira told it, when she became pregnant with him, she tried to abort his birth. Four children were enough, she said. She didn't want any more. She threw herself on the floor. This violent act didn't end the pregnancy but damaged his left ear and later made school difficult. This was compounded by the fact that the class was seated alphabetically and he was always in the back. "I never learned anything. My mother told everyone I was retarded, a *dummkopf*. She never believed any of us would succeed. Our parents never encouraged us. Only the strong could survive in that family."

Of the five children, only three were strong enough to survive their mother's constant taunts and sarcasm.

One of the strong ones was firstborn Rebecca, who was protected by the fact that she was carrying out her mother's wishes. Even in the early 1900s, when women rarely went to college, it was Sara's bold idea that her daughter become a medical doctor. It didn't discourage Sara that only a small number of women were admitted to medical schools. "You'll be the one who makes it," she told Rebecca when she showed signs of wavering.

I remember Aunt Beck, as we called Rebecca, as a short, stout woman with Sophie Tucker's physique and earthiness. Beck had a thriving general practice in the Bronx and ultimately was the studio doctor dispensing flu shots to the dancing teachers.

Arthur was strong enough to risk his mother's scorn and ridicule because he was as determined as she was. Caught up in the fever of dance excitement that swept the country in the early 1900s, Arthur realized that the public hungered for dancing instruction, and he was the one to provide it.

His mother viewed his first efforts to learn to dance quite differently. She had high hopes for this smart son of hers. He had a *Yiddishe kop*, a head for business like her own. And here he was spending half the night at a dance hall and sleeping the day away. She called him a dance bum, a no-goodnik, a good-for-nothing. But later, when he began contributing money to the household as an instructor at the prestigious Castle House dancing studio in New York, Sara quickly changed her mind about his dancing activities.

Two other children were not so lucky. Dave, a year younger than Arthur, was a gentle and fearful man. He hated working in the family's real estate venture—

collecting rents, dealing with the public—but could not stand up to his mother. Eventually he found his niche as legal counsel for the dancing studios.

George, born after Dave, was a nervous handsome boy who withered before his mother's bullying tactics. The tension between the two exploded when he married Henrietta, the daughter of a tailor. Sara had no use for Henrietta, Ira said. "As poor as we were, my mother was a rabbi's daughter and considered herself superior to tradesmen." George was torn between his love for his mother and his wife. Between the two of them, they destroyed him." George became manic-depressive and was eventually institutionalized.

Ira, the unwanted fifth child, was upbeat and cheerful all his long life. When my husband and I visited him, he often burst into song, told jokes. "The more my mother spoke against me, the more I believed in myself," he said. Ira had another source of strength that allowed him to shrug off his mother's belittling treatment. He had a close and loving relationship with his father. "He was a gentle good man. I inherited my positive attitude from him."

Sara judged her daughter-in-laws as pragmatically as if she were buying real estate, Dave's daughter told me. "Sara never approved of my mother, Sabina, because she wasn't rich and she wore glasses. On the other hand, Kathryn Kohnfelder, who was 18 when she married 31-year-old Arthur, won her mother-in-law's instant approval. She was young and pretty and her paternal grandfather came from Prague. Czechoslovakian Jews, like their German counterparts, were well-educated and successful. In contrast, Polish and Russian Jews were more often confined to the ghetto and led a threadbare existence.

As the undisputed head of the family, Sara was determined to keep her sons close to home. One by one, she managed to do just that. But the deceitful way in which Sara clipped Ira's wings almost took my breath away.

I only learned about this incident a few years ago when I visited Ira and his wife, Ann, in their tenth-floor condo in Hallandale, Florida. The light streamed in the picture windows overlooking the harbor. I sat on the couch while Ira, nearly 100 and wearing a cream-colored sports jacket, sat like a jockey astride his Barcalounger. As he spoke, I began to envision the fateful incident that occurred in 1923.

"At 18, I learned about a new invention, the electric radio that you plugged in the wall." This was revolutionary, he explained, because before, a radio was connected to a wet battery, and sometimes the battery overflowed and burned the floor. The electric radio had no such problems. Ira, yearning to be an entrepreneur, undoubtedly in response to his mother's taunts that he'd never amount to anything, got a bright idea: he'd go door-to-door demonstrating the wonders of this new invention.

But first he needed to locate a prosperous city whose residents could afford a new electric radio. That city, as his library research revealed, was Madison, Wisconsin.

In a saga befitting an aspiring Horatio Alger, Ira purchased a dilapidated Dodge touring car for $55. That was all the cash he had. His earnings, which totaled $600, had been appropriated by his mother for safekeeping. After a friend made necessary repairs on the car, Ira set out for Madison. It was July. The capital dome was surrounded by leafy trees. A fresh breeze blew off a nearby lake. There, he called on a company that sold radios and asked to see the owner, Mr. Bingham.

Mr. Bingham was impressed by Ira's plan to sell the new electric radio and asked him if he had any credit. Ira proudly described his nest egg of $600. The only thing that stood in the way of his new venture was a letter from his mother that Mr. Bingham requested. She needed only to confirm his savings and testify that he was reliable.

Ira had another bit of propitious news to relate to his mother. The owner had introduced him to the president of the bank, Mr. Westheimer, a well-respected and popular member of the community. Mr. Westheimer was also Jewish. "He has a beautiful daughter," Ira wrote to his mother, "He showed me her picture. But the problem is there are no eligible Jewish men in town." After a friendly conversation, Mr. Westheimer invited Ira to his house for dinner the following Friday evening.

Ira implored his mother to write a nice reference for him as soon as possible. Once Mr. Bingham received the letter he could start working. He knew he'd hit it off with the banker's daughter. His future was assured. Since his Yiddish-speaking mother could not write in English, he suggested that she enlist Arthur's help.

A week later, Mr. Bingham notified Ira that he had received a letter from Mrs. Teichman. Ira quickly sped over to the store. This time, the owner did not summon him to his office, but, busy with a customer, merely handed over the letter. With a sinking heart, Ira read the damning words in Arthur's flowing script. "My son has no savings. He is a spendthrift. He cannot be trusted with money."

I looked at Ira, his broad smile at odds with the incident he had just related.

"Weren't you angry?" I said, steaming at the deception that had occurred seventy years earlier. "That was a terrible thing to do."

"Sure, I was angry," Ira said, "I cried when I read the letter. But," he shrugged, "a mother is a mother. She knew if I married the banker's daughter, I'd never come home."

Sara had gotten her way once again.

CHAPTER 13

Moishe becomes Arthur Murray

Arthur's ambitions went beyond teaching dancing in Asheville.

Finally, the picture

emerged: the airless

tenements of Father's

impoverished boyhood

propelled him outward.

It was the quest for

a more rarified air.

Sara and Abraham, like almost all newcomers from eastern Europe in the late 1890s, settled on the Lower East Side of New York. Along with other immigrants, they were jammed into a square mile of tenements more densely populated than the slums of London or Bombay.

Browsing in the Library at Hebrew Union College in Cincinnati, I learned what living conditions were like when Abraham moved into a tenement in 1894.

Unadorned, utilitarian brick buildings, six to seven stories tall, were each arranged in the shape of a dumbbell. There were four apartments to a floor, two at each end of a narrow corridor. The front apartments were the only ones that got any light. These dumbbell tenements have been described as "great prison-like structures of brick, with narrow doors and windows, cramped passages and steep rickety stairs . . . in the middle is a foul-smelling place, supposed to do duty as an airshaft . . . they could not have been more villainously arranged to avoid any chance of ventilation . . . ."

Having lived his entire childhood in these airless dwellings, was it any wonder my father always insisted that a room have cross ventilation? Even years later, teachers at the New York studio were familiar with my father's demonstration. He would open two windows on adjacent walls and explain how this enabled the air to circulate.

Our family, checking into a hotel in the days when windows could be opened, invariably trooped from room to room, in search of one with cross ventilation. Led by a bellman, keys jangling, a resigned expression on his face, my father would reject one suite after another until he found one that met his specifications.

A social worker told my father not to take dancing seriously—advice unheeded.

The Teichmans' standard dumbbell tenement at 148 Suffolk Street bore no resemblance to the setting of *The Goldbergs*, which aired on radio in the 1930s and 40s. In this folksy story, Mrs. Goldberg yoo-hooed out the window to her neighbors. More than likely, the Teichmans had to pick their way through dense swarms of bedraggled half-washed immigrants, past overflowing garbage barrels and beneath tiers of fire escapes heaped with mattresses and pillows that served as beds on a hot night.

Sara and Abraham with their two small children, Rebecca and Moishe, struggled to subsist in their three-room rear apartment lit only by a dim gray light coming through one window. There was no electricity. A gas fixture that hung from the high kitchen ceiling had to be lit with a match and turned off at night. The kitchen was warmed by a black iron coal stove that also provided heat for baking and cooking. The bedrooms were unheated. In winter, children wore long-sleeved cotton underwear under layers of clothing.

I was aghast to learn from Ira that for four families there was only a sink with no hot water and one toilet. I made a quick calculation. The Teichmans had five children. If this was the norm, one toilet served twenty children and eight adults! I expressed my dismay at such an arrangement to Ira. "One bathroom for four families was better than the outhouse my parents were used to," he said.

Asheville debutantes and their mothers were eager to learn to dance from the elegant Arthur Murray. "I was the best dancer they had ever seen," he said.

Ira assured me that the family kept clean taking weekly baths in an old wash tub in the kitchen. They heated water for bathing on the stove. I tried to imagine what it was like, lifting that heavy kettle, pouring the boiling water in the tub. How many refills did it take for a decent bath? They used Octagon soap, a caustic product that rubbed the skin raw, Ira said.

My resourceful father found a way to augment home bathing, Ira said. He frequented a nearby bathhouse, a fixture in slum neighborhoods where a bath cost five cents, towel included. He then returned with wet hair, eluding his mother before she could question him about his evening activities.

During those early years in the new country before Ira was born, meals were mainly potatoes, cabbage, and soup. When Moishe was old enough he cooked for his three younger brothers, for breakfast rice boiled in milk, potato pancakes for dinner. I, too, simmer leftover rice in milk with raisins and cinnamon, which is tasty, but not the kind of fare to sustain a growing boy. No wonder my father said that his most vivid memory was a constant craving for meat, eggs, and sweets.

I was familiar with my father's predilection for sweets. When we went on a family trip he was constantly nibbling a Hershey bar or a Baby Ruth. He stashed candy bars in his bureau drawer and often produced one from the pocket of a sports jacket.

By the time that Ira, the youngest, was born, the family had begun to prosper. Moishe was then ten. Abraham bought the tenement they lived in for $500 and the family moved into a four-room front apartment. The kitchen overlooked the street, its pavement lined with stalls and pushcarts. A cacophony of voices drifted up through the open window. Rising above all others were the Yiddish dialects of eastern Europe.

"We ate in the kitchen," Ira said. "It was a large front room, with windows. We had a round table with gate legs. Mother served us; she didn't eat until everybody finished. There was always enough. When I played in the street, she threw down a piece of corn bread in a paper bag. The thick heavy farmer's bread was spread with shmaltz, chicken fat. It filled you up."

I asked Ira what street games they played. "There was boxball, using a soft rubber ball, and softball—here you hit the ball with your fist—and stick ball, using a stick as a bat." Ira had his own gang, five boys his age. "We'd fight with other children. When we had nothing to do we stole wood from the sweet potato man."

One day the street cleaners tore up the asphalt and left a temporary stockpile of rocks. Ira saw a chance to take over the other half of the block. He and his gang began throwing rocks, but the other gang had more rocks than they did.

"I ran to Arthur and asked him to help me. He refused. 'I'll only help you when there is another boy trying to hurt you. I won't help you when you start the fight.'"

At 12, Moishe was a serious boy, determined to make enough money to liberate his family from the squalor of the slums. "Arthur's role model in his struggle to become successful was his mother, whom he idolized," Ira said. "He observed her business practices, how she conducted a real estate deal."

At the same time, Moishe never got along with his father, Ira said. He ridiculed Abraham putting on his prayer shawl and reciting the Torah several times a day. "He wanted to show how religious he was," his son sneered.

One day when Phyllis and I were six or seven, my father told us the story of his father's promise of a gold watch. His voice still pulsated with anger.

When Moishe was 12, his father was eager for his son to be bar mitzvahed. To induce Moishe to attend religious school, Abraham promised him a gold watch when he graduated. So every day after school for close to a year, Moishe sat in the dark, musty classroom presided over by a rabbi who whipped the boys for any infraction.

Finally, he completed the hated schooling and ran home to receive his prize.

"Papa, my watch. You promised me a gold watch." Moishe held out his hand, clasped the watch, then excitedly opened his fingers to look at it. He looked again. It wasn't a gold watch; it was a cheap tin watch. In a rage, Moishe hurled the watch against the wall and ran out the door. He never forgave his father.

Dance history was made one cold January evening when gangly 14-year-old Moishe hesitantly opened the door of the Henry Street Settlement near his tenement. He scanned the list of classes—American history, literature, cooking—then found what he wanted: social dancing.

Mothers in Atlanta fought to get their children accepted into Arthur's dancing class. Within a year, the class totaled 1,000 youngsters.

Settlement houses, like the Henry Street Settlement, were a response to the flood of immigrants who began arriving in the 1880s. Social workers taught classes in a variety of subjects all designed to help "Americanize" these newcomers from eastern Europe and introduce them to a world removed from the crowded, garbage-strewn streets of the slums. The Henry Street Settlement was a leader in this field.

I can imagine Moishe that evening at the settlement house taking off his coat, folding it carefully while other boys carried on a conversation.

"Wotcha doin ear?" one said.

"Vot ya tink," the other answered with a wink. "Deres a goil in my readin class wid da begist tits ya ebba saw." No doubt, Moishe grimaced in disgust and redoubled his resolve to get out of the slums.

Originally, the teenage Moishe had one purpose in learning to dance—to be popular with girls. He was painfully shy. He stammered badly. It was agony to carry on a conversation with a girl. But on the dance floor he didn't have to talk and his partners often told him that he "danced good."

To practice his dancing, Moishe crashed wedding receptions held in public halls. These were mainly Italian and Polish groups, with women guests far outnumbering the men. Though uninvited, Moishe was always welcomed as an extra man. He enjoyed being fussed over by the women guests, mostly on the matronly side, and having his fill of wedding cookies and other sweets.

One year, after his lesson at the Henry Street Settlement, he won a waltz contest at a settlement house called the Amelia Sisterhood. A social worker, seeing Moishe's happy face, warned him dourly, "Now, don't take dancing seriously." This started him thinking. Until then, dancing had merely been a way of gaining poise and making friends. It occurred to him that perhaps dancing could be profitable.

Thus far, his efforts to make money had been a failure. A high school teacher had told him that he had some talent for drawing so he applied for a job with an architect—"a tightwad who said I could work for him without a salary."

A boy from the slums who attempted to escape from his environment needed to be tough. The young architects in the firm exchanged amused glances when Moishe brought out his salami sandwich in a brown paper bag. He clearly didn't belong. It was also likely that about this time, he had begun to be called "Murray," a common derivation of "Moishe." Many writers, in fact, reported that "Murray" was my father's given name.

Whatever the nomenclature, the time was ripe for an ambitious young man with a flair for ballroom dancing. "It was 1912 and the catchy beat of ragtime was just beginning to be heard in New York," my mother wrote. To appreciate the impact of the new jazz dancing, she pointed out that until 1900, few Americans danced and when they did it was usually stately quadrilles, decorous waltzes, and polkas.

The first decade of the 20th century transformed the dance floor, and by 1912, people of all ages were doing wacky dances with names like the Bunny Hug, Turkey Trot, and Grizzly Bear. It was during this dance craze that Moishe, an aspiring architect, carved out a new profession.

His first step was to apply for a job as an instructor at Grand Central Palace. This was a huge dance hall and the first place in the city to provide dancing partners at ten cents a dance. He had recently won a dance contest at the Palace and felt certain he qualified for the job. At the manager's instruction, Moishe picked a girl partner and waltzed sedately by. The manager shook his head and Moishe's heart sank. But the girl pleaded, "Oh, give the kid a break. I'll teach him the new dances," and thus his career was launched.

My father became an excellent dancer but soon realized that he knew very little about teaching dancing. His solution was a course of lessons at Castle House, a school managed by Irene and Vernon Castle, the outstanding society dance teachers of the era. The Castles, style-setters both in fashion and dancing, changed the entire direction of my father's life. He not only learned the graceful dances that the Castles popularized; he had his first glimpse of elegant society.

To pay for his tuition at Castle House, Moishe danced four hours a night at the dance hall. Combined with six hours of training at Castle House, he was dancing ten hours a day. His mother was appalled—the son with the *Yiddishe kop*, a head for business like her own, had become a dance bum. But he was sure enough of his direction to defy his powerful mother.

Events moved swiftly. When Baroness de Kuttleson, whom he had met at Castle House, asked him if he would be her partner at a resort hotel in Asheville, North Carolina, he accepted eagerly. Moishe Teichman, or Murray Teichman, wasted no time in becoming Arthur Murray. At this time when anti-Semitism, particularly directed at Eastern European Jews, was virulent, it would have been unthinkable to be Jewish when mixing with high society.

On my visit to Asheville a few years ago, I had a taste of the tightrope my father walked in creating a new persona as Arthur Murray. I became friends with a reporter there who offered to introduce me to a woman who had been in one of my father's dancing classes for children. Mrs. B., who resembled Katharine Hepburn, and I had a good chat, that is, until the reporter said to Mrs. B., "Did you know that Arthur Murray was Jewish?" Mrs. B. paled and was unable to respond for what seemed like several minutes.

My father was social director at the Battery Park Hotel, which seemed a perfect setting to be dramatized in a musical. The scrapbook in which he painstakingly pasted the clippings of social events at the elite hotel described a constant round of dinner dances, tea dances, and costume balls. Ladies wore gowns of embroidered silk chiffon or satin with elaborately draped overskirts. As the orchestra sounded its catchy ragtime tune, all eyes were on Miss Charlotte Dupont, the debutante of the year, and Mr. Murray.

Judging by the society editor's effusive remarks, Mr. Murray was very popular with members of Southern society. Photographs show a tall, thin, dark-eyed young man, dressed in tails or a dinner jacket, gravely demonstrating the maxixe (a Brazilian tango), the hesitation, one step, or lulu-fado with a debutante or society matron.

While enjoying luxurious living at the Battery Park, Arthur never forgot his family. He began sending money home every week. Eventually, through Arthur's funds, his three brothers received college educations. Ira, who described himself as a "kid brother," recalled that Arthur gathered the funnies left each week in the hotel lobby and sent them to Ira.

Arthur, conscious of his age, then 19, had recently grown a moustache in an effort to look older. On his first evening at the hotel, the baroness led him to the card room and introduced him to the grande dame of Asheville. "Mrs. Vanderbilt, may I present my new partner, Arthur Murray." Edith Vanderbilt raised her pince-nez and studied the new instructor. "Young man," she said, "shave off that ridiculous moustache!"

In later years, my father managed a flourishing dancing studio in Manhattan. Woe to the teacher who sported a beard or moustache or smoked a pipe. All three, he said, revealed a man's lack of self-confidence.

Despite a rocky start, Arthur quickly became Mrs Vanderbilt's favorite dancing partner and a frequent guest at Biltmore House. Mrs. Vanderbilt urged him to take his pick of any of the splendid horses from the celebrated Vanderbilt stable. I recall my father often massaging the little finger of his right hand. He had broken his finger jumping one of the thoroughbreds, he said.

At Biltmore House, Arthur taught young Cornelia Vanderbilt the currently popular dance, the lulu-fado. After the lesson, he frequently had a nice dinner. But where did the young man dine? I pondered this question touring Biltmore House a few years ago. Did Arthur eat with the Vanderbilts in the breakfast room, elegant with its tooled leather wall covering. (There, contrary to the name "breakfast room," the family had most of their meals). Or was Arthur relegated to the downstairs servants' dining room? This was a somber looking room with walls painted brown and furnished with a mahogany dining table and caned bentwood chairs.

As expected, Phyllis and I were not interested in whether Arthur dined upstairs or downstairs. What intrigued us was my father's remark that he had fallen in love with an Asheville society girl.

"Why didn't you marry her?" we chimed.

"I couldn't bring her home to my mother," he said quietly. A Yiddish-speaking mother would have been an embarrassment.

And then Arthur met Kathryn.

"She was the only Jewish flapper I ever knew," he said.

CHAPTER 14

When Arthur meets Kathryn

Kathryn and Arthur off on their European honeymoon.

He met her at a

Newark radio station.

She was vivacious

and he was, well,

Arthur Murray.

In time, she became

his essential partner.

At the time Kathryn and Arthur met, in 1925, my father had just returned to New York after his enormous success dancing his way through Asheville society and had emerged as an elegant dancer. No one in this circle of aristocratic Southerners suspected that Arthur Murray was Moishe Teichman, raised in the slums of New York's Lower East Side.

His job at the exclusive Asheville resort was followed by several years in Atlanta where he organized dancing classes for children from families on the social register. He called these classes Club de Vingt. He had no idea that *vingt* meant "twenty," but the *Atlanta Journal's* society editor, his newfound mentor, assured him that it sounded exclusive. After one year, he had a thousand youngsters enrolled in his classes.

Mother's family called him "Mr. Murray"—until the night his car wouldn't start.

He was 29, rapidly becoming famous as a dancing teacher, when he had an impromptu meeting at a New Jersey radio station. She was 18 years old, studying to be a schoolteacher. He was reserved with a stammer. She was sassy, flirtatious—much like the Southern girls he admired. He had lived among Southern socialites for the past decade. She had never left Booraem Avenue in Jersey City.

Their meeting took place at WOR in Newark. Kathryn's best friend, Peggy Muller, whose boyfriend was a director at the station, invited Kathryn to a broadcast that featured a popular jazz band. Kathryn had never been to a radio station and was excited at the prospect. On the bus ride over, Peggy told her friend that she was going to meet Arthur Murray.

"Who's he?" Kathryn asked.

"Why, haven't you seen those big ads with the footprints?" Peggy answered. The dotted footprints illustrated how to place one's feet in a dance step. Yes, Katie had seen them but she didn't think the man with the footprints was real.

At the station, the band played a number and the man who was to become my father—slim and dignified in a dinner jacket—stepped up to the microphone and introduced himself.

"I'm Arthur Murray," he said in his high-pitched voice. He spoke in a stammer, spelling his name letter by letter, which was the custom in the early days of radio. When he called for volunteers among the studio audience to act as students, my mother jumped up immediately, flashing him a smile.

As the dance lesson ended and general dancing began, Arthur approached Kathryn, introduced himself in his courtly manner, and asked her to dance. Kathryn was wearing a dress that a neighbor had made from a remnant of velvety green duvetyn. It was modeled on a form-fitting Russian tunic and held together with snaps. At his invitation, she threw open her arms, whereupon the dress unsnapped in front. She hurriedly snapped the dress again, and they danced.

Kathryn had no concerns about her proficiency on the dance floor; she was known as the best dancer in her set. But no compliments came from Arthur. "Instead," she recalled, "Arthur asked me to remove my hand from his neck and place it on the back of his shoulder."

At the end of their first dance, Kathryn said brightly, "Now I'll have something to tell my grandchildren." Arthur claimed he thought at the time "our grandchildren," but was too shy to say it.

In her book, my mother described the ups and downs of their whirlwind courtship. One episode that reminded me of the radio soap operas I used to listen to is how an ingrown toenail almost ended their romance. After turning down a midweek date with Arthur—she was too embarrassed to tell him she was only allowed to go out on weekends—she happily accepted a Saturday night date. All was well until Kathryn developed a painful ingrown toenail, probably resulting from the short, high-heeled, vamp shoes she loved to wear. When the toe became so painful she could hardly walk, she phoned Arthur and said she was sick—a sore toe was too unattractive to mention. Whatever the excuse, this second brush-off was the last straw for Arthur. A week of silence passed. Kathryn wrote Arthur a penitent note explaining about the toe and saying that she hoped to see him. He called at once and invited her to dinner and a Broadway show.

For my father, who was familiar with Manhattan, Jersey City was unknown territory. He had no intention of inconveniencing himself making a trip to pick her up, but when it became obvious that his youthful date expected to be called for, he resignedly wrote down directions to Booraem Avenue.

On a January evening in 1925, Arthur drove up to the Kohnfelders' two-family house in a black Rolls Royce. Neighbors peered out their windows. Lenore, Kathryn's mother, answered the door. She was an auburn-haired beauty with a porcelain complexion. That evening, in a green velveteen dress, she looked her best. Abe, Kathryn's father, the fun-loving newspaper man, offered the proper young man a drink of Prohibition gin mixed with grape juice. Although Arthur never drank he took a sip, gulped, and asked for some sugar. As the story went, Kathryn's father whispered to his daughter, "He's okay, baby. Anybody who puts sugar in a drink is safe to go out with."

Family introductions over, Arthur took Kathryn to dinner at the Vanderbilt Hotel on Park Avenue, then popular with members of the southern aristocracy. Kathryn, in her hastily acquired wardrobe, was well aware of the attractive young women who waved white gloved hands at her escort. A pretty honey-voiced woman in a stylish flounced dress stopped by their table. "Why, Arthur, it's been ages since we've seen you. And who is this charming young lady?"

I can imagine my mother managing a bright smile and, with a pang of envy, noting the socialite's smart outfit.

Arthur had two tickets to *No, No Nanette*, starring Ruby Keeler. This was the most sought-after play on Broadway, but Arthur's mind was on their conversation, not Ruby Keeler's tap dancing.

Kathryn peppered her date with probing questions about the dancing business. The shy young man began talking. Kathryn hardly said ten words. He talked and talked. They missed the opening curtain and eventually the entire play. As Arthur reached for the check, he remarked, "We have so much to talk about, we should get married."

On their second date, Arthur took Kathryn to the Riding Club on 67th Street frequented by New York society. They were there to take part in an equestrian "music ride," a routine as intricate as a quadrille. Having learned horsemanship in Asheville, Arthur felt right at home. Kathryn's riding experience consisted of a few hours on a tired nag at a stable in Belmar, New Jersey, where the Kohnfelders had a summer cottage on the shore.

Upstairs in the ladies dressing room, self-assured young women were changing into riding clothes. Kathryn slipped on her brown tweed jacket and brown whipcord jodhpurs—an outfit she had wheedled from her father—only to discover that the other women wore black fitted jackets with velvet collars and white stocks. Once in the ring, the riding exercise was a nightmare. Kathryn's horse, sensing her inexperience and fright, reared up and bucked. The ringmaster shouted at her and finally asked her to leave the ring. Arthur, unaware of her trials, was chatting with his friends while he executed the complicated figures of the music ride.

Kathryn crept up to the dressing room and cried. Remembering the humiliating riding scene brought a fresh flood of tears. But once she got into her high heels and flapper gown and blue velvet cape—another purchase she had induced her father to buy—she was ready for a gala evening. She was sure Arthur would suggest going to a nightclub; she had never been to one. But to her disappointment, Arthur proposed driving to her house and making egg

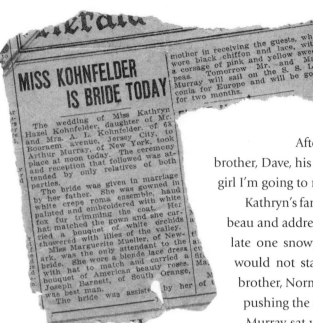

The bride, a mere 18 years old, fibbed about her age. She told her husband-to-be she was 20.

sandwiches. He explained that after years of living in hotels, this was a great treat for him.

After this second date he called his brother, Dave, his family confident, saying, "I've met the girl I'm going to marry!"

Kathryn's family was a little awed by her prominent beau and addressed him as Mr. Murray—that is, until late one snowy night when Arthur's car froze and would not start. Kathryn woke up her father and brother, Norman, and together they got soaking wet pushing the car through snow and slush while Mr. Murray sat warm and dry at the wheel. After this, the Kohnfelder men felt sufficiently comfortable calling my mother's beau "Arthur."

The next day, Arthur returned with elaborate gifts for the family and broached his intentions to marry Kathryn. "Arthur," Abe Kohnfelder said, "We think the world of you. But we feel that Kathryn is a *lit-tle* young for marriage."

Kathryn held her breath during this discussion of her age. She had fibbed to Arthur that she was 20, not 18. Kathryn needn't have worried. Arthur, unperturbed by his future father-in-law's objections, described his plan for an April wedding and a three-month honeymoon in Europe. As generally happened, Arthur had his way.

What attracted Arthur to Kathryn? He marveled at her poise, her sparkle—the way a roomful of people leaned toward her like flowers following the sun.

When Kathryn met Arthur she was attending State Normal School in Newark, New Jersey. A two-year certificate would enable her to teach school. A giddy flapper, as she described herself, she frequently played hooky from normal school.

Often, she hung out at a Greenwich Village joint called Cushman's, which attracted the college crowd. She was 18. One night, mustering her courage, she walked over to the pianist and asked him to play a new song called "the Charleston."

In my mind's eye, she leaned over the piano in her short, pleated skirt with an overblouse and a low slung belt, looking like a flapper in a John Held drawing. A final touch was her striped, barber-pole stockings and unbuckled, black galoshes.

To the refrain of "Charleston, Charleston," she performed the new dance. The crowd clapped and imitated Kathryn's swiveling footwork. Before long, the room was a sea of waving arms and kicking legs. The piano player pounded out the rhythm: *There's nothing finer than the Charleston, Charleston . . . .*

In later years, friends of mine who met my mother still recalled her songs, many from vaudeville, and her jokes. Bill, one of these friends, often launched into what was then considered one of Kathryn's risque jokes.

"When Bill visited us in Honolulu, the city had just installed a new bus line," Kathryn said. "We couldn't get on the first time. The second time, they were still mobbed. Finally, the third time, we squeezed our way on board. When I saw the conductor coming our way, I tried to find my money. I hated to keep him waiting but it was so crowded I couldn't find my change purse. Finally the man next to me says, 'Madam, *I'll* pay your bus fare. You've unzipped my fly three times!'"

Kathryn's father, Abe, taught her to perform. At an early age, he relinguished school for a stint in vaudeville. Vaudeville might not have paid much but it left the ebullient Abe with a legacy of songs that he taught to Kathryn. Family members and friends go misty-eyed recalling Kathryn, an edge of the Joisey tramp in her voice, singing such songs as "The Cat's Meow." Even at 90, when dementia threatened to destroy her personality, she could still sing all the verses of "Frankie and Johnny" and recall the entirety of "The Shooting of Dan McGrew."

Unlike Kathryn, a winning entertainer, Arthur was not much fun. His speech was hesitant, and he stammered frequently. Despite his lack of skill at telling jokes, he kept on trying. When my parents retired to Honolulu and became inveterate party-givers, my father carried a little black book in his sport jacket to carefully record jokes that he wished to add to his repertoire.

For a young man who wanted nothing to do with Judaism, my father undoubtedly felt the Kohnfelders were a perfect fit as prospective in-laws. My grandparents were Jewish but I don't recall their ever mentioning Judaism. Contrary to the ghetto where my father's family lived, my mother grew up on a leafy street in Jersey City. Neighbors were mainly German Catholic and Irish families. Kathryn's religious education consisted of attending various churches with her girlfriends.

One of the things Kathryn and Arthur had in common was ambition. He knew where he was going. She knew she wanted to be a part of his plans. On that first date at the Vanderbilt Hotel, he poured out his plans for the dancing studio. At some point, I imagine he looked into her velvety brown eyes fastened on him and thought, *We could go through life together.*

Their wedding announcement in the *Jersey Observer* was puzzling. It didn't sound as if it were written by my grandfather, a newspaper man. There was no mention of where the wedding took place or who officiated. Instead, the fragile yellowed clipping described what the bride wore: "She was gowned in white crepe roma ensemble, hand painted and embroidered with white fox fur trimming the coat. Her hat matched the gown and she carried a bouquet of white orchids showered with lilies of the valley."

It surprised me that only a handful of relatives attended the ceremony. I would have expected my sociable grandfather to invite Mr. Ealy and other big shots of the *Observer*. And what about my grandfather's two sisters and their husbands. Wouldn't he want to show off a son-in-law who drove a Rolls Royce?

My guess is that my father didn't want the Kohnfelders to spend a lot of money on their daughter's wedding. For one thing, he regarded Abe as a poor businessman who might find himself in dire straits. More to the point, he considered large weddings a waste of money. "You spend a thousand dollars or more on a ceremony that takes an hour," he said. To my father, who lacked the usual sentiment, it made perfect sense.

My grandfather undoubtedly protested the spartan wedding that Arthur had planned. "I'd do anything for my little girl," he said, but few people won an argument with my father. The only attendant to the bride was Kathryn's best friend, Peggy, who was responsible for their meeting. Best man was Joseph Barnett of South Orange, a name that seems to have been picked out of a hat. I've never heard the name; no one has ever mentioned him.

The day after the wedding, my parents boarded the *S.S. Laconia*, a Cunard ocean liner, for a three-month honeymoon in Europe. My publicity-minded father had already notified the press. A newspaper photo showed the couple on shipboard demonstrating a dance step. My mother was dressed in a simple fashionable dress, a cloche hat framed her face. She wore a blasé expression that belied her 18 years.

In London, Kathryn met a girl named Marjorie, who was also on her honeymoon, and the two of them pranced down Regent Street in black dinner jackets; one wielded a lorgnette, the other sported a monocle and cane. There were lavish dinners hosted by dancing masters with titled connections.

In her book, my mother described a formal luncheon at a country estate that she felt needed livening up. She obliged by playing and singing several stanzas of "The Cat's Meow." Mother wrote: "With my cracked voice and New Joisy twang, the English guests couldn't understand a word."

By coincidence I recently came across the sheet music for this song, dated 1922.

Alone in my study, carefully handling the pages, I mouthed the lyrics sounding, I thought, like my mother at 18 impersonating a girl from Brooklyn. *It was love at foist sight when I met him that night his lamps looked into me heart.* I felt tearful that Mother was no longer with us and picked up the phone to call my sister.

Despite the hijinks and elegant dinners, the honeymoon was not a success. Kathryn missed her family—she had never been away from home before. Knowing my parents' temperament, both compulsive achievers, day after day of unplanned activity while getting used to each other's ways was no doubt a trial for both. Perhaps most important, Kathryn was accustomed to a father who was demonstrative, given to hugs. Leaving for work, Abe always kissed his wife, Lenore. My father was stiff, reserved, unaccustomed to expressing his feelings. My father only kissed my sister and me when we were departing on a trip or returning from one.

When the *S. S. Laconia* docked in New York, Kathryn rushed down the gangplank and into a waiting cab. She fled to her parents' place at Belmar. Arthur stayed in New York for two days, then followed Kathryn to the shore.

"I was never so glad to see anyone," Kathryn wrote. She and my father returned to their apartment in New York, and whatever my mother's private sorrows, they remained held properly beneath the surface. At least for a time.

CHAPTER 15

Kathryn swings from a chandelier

Kathryn, under the lights.

The rising new

medium of television

was great for Father's

business. But it made

Mother a star.

Father was best

behind the scenes.

The early '50s ushered in the Golden Age of Comedy when millions of Americans roared with laughter over the antics of such comedians as Milton Berle, Lucille Ball, Red Skelton, and Jackie Gleason. These stars, who had honed their skills in vaudeville, were the competition that my parents faced when my father bought time on CBS for a weekly summer series. Neither my father or mother had any theatrical experience but that didn't faze my father. Arthur, who was known as the world's leading dancing teacher, had made his name selling dancing by mail. He knew what the public wanted. He also recognized that Kathryn was a natural performer.

My mother's role had changed over the quarter century since she had married my father. She was no longer the outsider at the dancing studio, the scared little mouse that she had been as an 18-year-old newlywed. With my sister and I tucked away at boarding school, Kathryn had found her niche writing teachers' manuals for my father's business and regaling audiences at womens' clubs with "Arthur" stories.

It was at a Hadassah event where I first saw my mother in action. A sea of women's faces looked expectantly up at her. Mother smiled winsomely at her audience and said, "Arthur stopped in at my office last week. 'I've just bought time on CBS to give dancing lessons,' he said. 'The program starts tomorrow.'

"'That's nice,' I said. 'Are you going to teach a dancing lesson?'

"'No,' he said, 'You are.'

"'But Arthur, I can't be on television. I'm not beautiful like Faye Emerson or Audrey Meadows or Betty Furness.'

"'That doesn't matter,' he said. 'The screen is so small and the reception is so poor no one will be able to tell the difference.'"

She laughed along with her audience.

Father was appalled at how badly TV studios were lit. He would quickly change that.

My parents' first TV show was no laughing matter. Hank and I watched it on our newly purchased seventeen-inch screen. On a dimly lit set, Mother sat at a desk, then stood up awkwardly to teach the box step, which she demonstrated with a male instructor. A Victrola provided the dance music. As we squinted at flickering black-and-white images, we had no idea that color television was only a few years away. Now and then Hank fiddled with the dial to get rid of the snow. When the show was over, neither of us spoke for a few minutes.

"Feel like a little ice cream?" I said, trying to lighten the moment.

My father wasn't concerned about the stiff dancing—he knew how to stage a dance number. What disturbed him was the lighting, which made his pretty wife look gaunt and hollow-eyed. He quickly determined that the so-called lighting experts were useless and set out to discover how to light a subject himself. He conferred with Hal Phyfe, a leading society photographer, who imparted the secret of flattering camera photography, which was the use of overhead lighting, a technique that concealed pouches and wrinkles.

My most vivid memory of this early phase of the show was of my father rushing around the set barking orders—"Forget about showing their feet; people want to see their faces!" My father fired "experts" and directors one after another and soon became known as "the monster of television." To use one of my mother's favorite expressions, "He was as shy as a barracuda." All this changed when Coby Ruskin, a rumpled, stage-wise director, appeared on the scene.

In normal times, Ruskin, a brilliant director and actor, might not have considered taking a job on *The Arthur Murray Party*. My father, the producer, had a reputation for being difficult, and his wife was a rank amateur with stage aspirations. But these were not normal times. This was the shameful era in the 1950s when a Wisconsin senator, Joseph McCarthy, launched a campaign to rid the entertainment industry of those he considered Communists. A brilliant career could be ruined by a mention in *Red Channels*, a booklet that claimed to document Communist influence in radio and television.

Arthur hit a high note when he became a television producer. Everybody had a good time at *The Arthur Murray Party*.

My father, who was rabid on the subject of Communists and believed Coby was "one of them," nevertheless had no qualms about hiring this seasoned director. Coby recognized my mother's gift for comedy and under his coaching she held her own with such pros as Bert Lahr, Groucho Marx, and Robert Cummings. That was enough for Arthur.

Unlike many performers, Mother never used cue cards and rarely flubbed a line—except on one occasion. She was doing the Bayer aspirin commercial. She had given this spiel so many times her mind suddenly went blank, but she recovered gracefully. Smiling at the camera, she said, "You know, our son-in-law is a doctor and he always keeps Bayer aspirin in his medicine cabinet."

Hank groaned and glared at me as we watched the rest of the show. "You're going to have to tell your mother that this could get me into serious trouble." At the time, a doctor could be brought up on charges by the medical society for something as innocuous as having his name mentioned in the popular press.

With mischievous delight, my father refused to take Hank's situation seriously. One day, Hank was flippng through the *New York Post* when, to his horror, he found a cartoon of two doctors in operating room garb. The caption read: "Arthur Murray's son-in-law said, 'May I cut in?'"

While my parents' burgeoning notoriety was painful for Hank, it opened up a new world for Kathryn. Television made Kathryn Murray a star. Having lunch with Mother one day at the Women's Exchange, the hostess led us to our table. I followed Mother, her red cloth coat swinging about her legs, black suede pumps clicking on the tile floor. I was conscious of heads turning, whispers of, "There's Kathryn Murray!" Seated, Mother smiled at me and gamely tried to focus on our conversation.

For so many years, she hadn't fit in. She had been an outsider at the dancing studio, even in her own home where Helen was more of a mother to us than she. Now the adulation glowed in her face even though she disguised her pleasure with a string of self-deprecatory remarks.

"Almost invariably when I get into a taxi, the driver recognizes me by my voice, not by my face. 'Say, you're Kathryn Murray, aren't you?' a cabbie said. I answered, 'Why, yes,' and waited, pleased and a little shy, for some remark about the show. He said, 'I knew it. I'd know that voice anywhere—the voice with a crack in it.'"

When Coby introduced pantomime numbers for my mother, I saw my big chance to write for television. The demands of the skit were simple—my mother played a winsome character each week, such as the little tramp or a Southern belle. The plot need only lead into a dance number.

I loved thinking up pantomime ideas—I could do this while taking Phil and Peter for a walk. I sent a stream of skit ideas to Coby each week and never heard from anyone unless the writers were unable to come up with a pantomime number.

Then one of the staff phoned me and casually told me they were using my skit. I felt like a poor relative, as if the professionals begrudged having to use material from an outsider.

I never discussed my role as a scriptwriter with my mother. I knew she wouldn't want anything to impinge on her relationship with Coby. The thrill for me was having an idea percolate in my head and within a few days, that idea appeared on television screens in thousands of homes.

In addition, the pay seemed enormous for an idea that I could develop while brushing my teeth. The first skit that I sold to the show netted me $250, which in those days was a woman's average monthly salary.

By this time, the pint-sized 58-year-old grandmother had already gained a tremendous following, particularly among women her age or older. "She's so natural," women said to me. Kathryn loved doing daredevil stunts. She swung from a chandelier, careened on roller skates, performed pratfalls and somersaults. I thought my father should be more concerned about her safety. In one of her skits a horse stomped on her instep. My father dismissed my concerns. "Fans identify themselves with Kathryn. The more daring the stunt, the younger her fans feel," he explained.

Kathryn had good reason for looking adoringly at her husband. *The Arthur Murray Party* had made her a star.

Despite her daring persona on television, Kathryn was the traditional housewife of a postwar era that extolled domesticity. Women were not supposed to have careers. In my suburban New York neighborhood I knew only one mother, Robin, who worked outside the home. Robin was a copyeditor at an advertising agency, which I thought sounded challenging and fun. But I wouldn't have had the guts. Whenever anything went amiss with Robin's children, her neighbors blamed it on her job:

"That son of hers is headed for trouble. If she would only stay home and greet her children with milk and cookies."

Women's editors advised women to prepare themselves for the arrival of their husbands each night. "Touch up your makeup, put a ribbon in your hair, and be fresh-looking," they wrote. Kathryn confided in interviews how she "snagged" her husband and described "What makes an ideal wife?" A petite powerhouse, she baked cookies at 6 a.m. and kept a filled cookie tin on Arthur's desk at the office.

Her fans told me that the high point of the television show was the romantic ending: dressed in a bouffant evening gown, Kathryn stepped forward and said with a smile, "To put a little fun in your life, try dancing." She held out her arms and, to the strains of a Vienna waltz, Arthur swooped her away.

Her fans would have been shocked to learn that instead of whispering sweet nothings in her ear, Arthur was apt to be criticizing some minor mishap of the show. She gave a stellar performance every week, but he never stopped finding fault.

Any criticism from my father caused my mother to wither instantly. Surprisingly, she never fought back, never disputed his pronouncements. Ordinarily, she was a feisty lady, very much in charge. She had no hesitation about interfering in *her* parents' lives: "Daddy, don't you think it's time you retired?" Or, "Daddy, have you cut out the booze?" But she reacted like a little girl to any criticism from her husband. He needed only to look disapprovingly at the dress she wore. "Everything you wear looks the same," he might say, and she would rush out to confer with Valentina, her favorite designer. Hawk-eyed, Daddy watched over her drinking. Dining with friends at a restaurant, he had no compunction at calling across the table, "Madam, you've had enough!" At such times, she set down her wine glass and gave him a contrite smile.

Lucy Ruskin, Coby's wife, revealed the unhappy consequence of Arthur's behavior. "I recall telephone conversations with Kathryn at 1 or 2 o'clock in the morning," Lucy told me. "She probably had a few drinks in her. She would call Coby and he'd try to console her about Arthur's constant harrangue. 'Why don't you leave him, Katie? You're a woman of means. On the other hand, if you want to be Mrs. Arthur Murray, then you don't leave him'. She felt that without Arthur she would lose some kind of identity."

Amazingly, Mother's despair over Daddy's criticism didn't affect her performance. In fact, *The Arthur Murray Party* that started off as a summer replacement was now in demand as a top-rated show. A sure sign of success was in 1952 when *The Arthur Murray Party* acquired General Foods as a sponsor. "It was a shock to the trade to have Arthur, a former sponsor, hired as talent," she said.

Today, dance contests have become the main attraction of top-ranking shows such as *Dancing with the Stars*, but in 1956, when my father dreamed up the idea of a celebrity dance contest for the Murray show, almost everyone, including Coby and my mother, thought it was corny.

"Arthur, I can't ask Helen Hayes to do a jitterbug," Kathryn said. But Arthur was right. After several dancing lessons, the First Lady of the American Theatre was delighted to participate, and soon the celebrity dance contest become the main attraction of the Murray show. Ratings zoomed. When my parents retired in 1960, their show's ratings outstripped Lawrence Welk's.

Kathryn limbers up before one of her daredevil numbers.

But success exerted a price. The strain of producing an hour-long show every week for the previous ten years exacerbated my mother's drinking problem and led to her second suicide attempt.

One evening in the late 1950s, they filmed the television show that marked ten years of *The Arthur Murray Party*. They were both tired. Afterward, they hurried through the theater, tossing perfunctory thank you's to Jeanie, the make-up girl, choreographer June Taylor, and Mike, one of the cameramen.

Coby was waiting for Kathryn outside her dressing room, a grin on his face. "Don't tell anybody, but I think you stole the show from Groucho."

"Was I really okay?" she asked in her little girl voice.

"Madam, let's go," Arthur said irritably.

In the darkness of the long black limo on the way to their weekend house next to ours in Rye, New York, they sat in silence. My father's querulous voice broke the silence.

"Why did you let Joey Bishop stay on so long?" he asked. I can imagine what he said next. "He's not funny. He didn't get a single laugh." My mother didn't answer.

An hour later, I heard a crunch of gravel and saw the arc of headlights as the limo circled the driveway. I waited for Mother's customary call, eager to tell her how good she was in the skit with Groucho. I glanced at the clock several times, feeling a growing uneasiness.

Finally, I called her myself. "You were wonderful. That skit with Groucho was a scream."

"Your father said I let Joey Bishop stay on too long," she said. Her voice was flat.

I could feel my irritation growing. "Joey Bishop—who cares? The show was wonderful."

My mother continued in the same monotone. "Daddy said he wasn't funny. He didn't get any laughs."

"Mother, you know how Daddy is—he's never satisfied."

I hung up feeling uneasy. A week earlier, Phyllis told me that Mother kept vodka in plastic bottles in her cosmetic kit. Had she taken more than a few sips?

While I was debating what to do, the phone rang. It was my father and he sounded frightened. "Your mother has taken an overdose of sleeping pills. I can't wake her. Is Hank there?"

Hank called for an ambulance and made arrangements for my mother to be admitted at Lenox Hill Hospital in New York. After the emergency crew carried Mother on a stretcher into the ambulance, Hank slipped into the driver's seat of my father's Lincoln Continental.

"I'll drive, Arthur," Hank said, holding out his hand for the keys. As we sped to the hospital, now and then streetlights shone on my father's tense but impassive face. No one spoke. No one patted Arthur's shoulder and assured him Mother would be all right. No one asked my father what had provoked Mother's action.

When we arrived at the hospital, the doctor told us that they had passed a tube through Mother's nose and into her stomach to wash out the remains of the sleeping pills. She came home the next day. Strange as it seems, the incident was never discussed.

4
Taking a second look

CHAPTER 16

A daughter's lament

Kathryn in the Honolulu penthouse.

Mother and I were very much alike, but I never felt comfortable with her. Perhaps because she was never comfortable with herself.

My mother is in my bones. I look in the mirror and see her mouse-like face as she appeared in her elder years when her hair was white, like mine is now. Studying my reflection, I think of the many times I've assumed my mother's supplicating expression, as if to say "I mean well."

Over the years, my mother often signed her letters to Phyllis and me, "Miss Meanwell," with a drawing of a smiley face. When she bought us outfits that weren't becoming or didn't fit, she hung her head like a little girl. *I meant well.*

We were alike in many other ways. When I'm "low-spirited"—my mother's expression for her bouts of depression—I speak in her flat, monotone voice. I catch myself rummaging through my purse to make sure I have my keys, as she did when dementia first struck. At the time, she was a widow living in the penthouse in Honolulu. One night before we went out to dinner, she sat with a purse on her lap and fingered her keys and other items over and over with the intensity of a woman saying her rosary. By then it was too late to make contact with her. She was already gone.

Could I have done more over the years to bring us closer? Could I have helped her cope with her bouts of depression?

There were rules: A good front, a brave face. She could charm a room, though.

My mother had very little mothering. Her mother, Lenore, doted on Norman, Kathryn's older brother, and hardly noticed her daughter. Helen, the family helper, would curl Kathryn's hair in corkscrews and tell her she looked like Mary Pickford, but it didn't make up for a mother's love.

She loved to perform with her charismatic father, the one-time vaudevillian, but invariably she was left alone when Abe joined his buddies at his Jersey City neighborhood pub.

My mother is in my bones. I even sound like her. People often said to me, "If I weren't looking at you I'd swear I was talking to Kathryn Murray." Some of her favorite expressions keep popping into my mouth. The other day, saying goodbye to a friend, I found myself saying "Be of good cheer," a Kathrynism.

So why, even though we were so much alike, was I never able to get close to my mother? There were plenty of moments that could have brought us closer.

One of these moments was the time I fell in love with a young man named David. One spring morning, home from Sarah Lawrence on Easter vacation, I was finishing my oatmeal in the small dining room of my parents' two-bedroom Park Avenue apartment in New York. I was still dressed in my nightgown and bathrobe. My mother breezed in trailing a whiff of Arpegé. She perched on one of the Chippendale chairs and I saw she was wearing what I had come to think of as her office uniform, a Valentina black wool dress, a gold necklace and earrings from Tiffany.

"Dear, was the boy you went out with in Wisconsin named 'David Chatfield?'"

Yes, I said. I scanned my mother's face with a chill of apprehension. Why was she asking me about David?

In her pretty gowns and with her pretty face, Kathryn was always the hit of "The Arthur Murray Party."

I had met David, a rangy intellectual New Englander at summer school at the University of Wisconsin when I was 18. A school friend had given my name to him. It was July of 1944. One afternoon, he called on the dorm phone. That evening, there he was, in the dimly lit hallway, a towering lean figure who from the start took my breath away. His warm brown eyes and boyish smile had captivated me.

I was abruptly drawn back to the present when Mother said she had something to show me. I followed her into the living room. We sat on the bold floral print couch, which bore Dorothy Draper's bright signature colors and always made me feel a little sick.

Mother ordinarily left for her office at the dancing studio by nine, but today she had delayed her departure to talk to me. Her eyes looked pityingly at me. And then I noticed the clipping on her lap that she had neatly scissored from the society page of *The New York Times*. She handed me the clipping. It was a photo of someone called Emily Whitman, a grave-looking young woman.

What did this have to do with me? I read on. "Mr. and Mrs. Olcott Whitman, of Wellesley, Massachusetts, announce the engagement of their daughter to David Chatfield, son of Mr. and Mrs. Taylor Chatfield of Amherst, Massachusetts." I suddenly felt sweaty in my quilted robe. Tears pricked my eyes.

"I'm so sorry," my mother said, giving me a beseeching look.

Heartsick, I wanted to tell my mother how magical that summer had been. I wanted to tell her that I always knew it was a summer romance, that David was destined to marry a girl who was his own kind—one from a family of scholars who spoke in precise cultivated voices. But most of all I wanted a mother who would take me in her arms and let me have a good cry.

But Mother jumped to her feet. Her heels sank into the plush carpet. "Dear, you need to get out. Why don't you take a dancing lesson?" She gave my cheek a perfunctory pat, her face reflecting concern. Reluctant to leave me alone, she said, "Shall we have lunch a little later at the Women's Exchange? They have a delicious crabmeat salad."

She pulled on her gray spring coat and gathered her gloves and purse. "I'll call you when I get to the office." The front door closed behind her.

My mother is in my bones. She was always in motion. The day after I gave birth to my first child, Mother visited me at the hospital, then a time when birthing mothers enjoyed a leisurely week in the hospital. I sat in bed feeling languorous. Conscious of the sensation of my newly full breasts, I speculated whether it was time to nurse. I looked forward to the strangely sexual stimulation of my baby sucking my nipples.

My mother knocked. She swept in, smiling, wearing her American Beauty red wool coat, wafting a perfume she said was "Joy." "Daddy gave me a bottle," she said. "It's a litttle overwhelming." She smiled. "How are you, Baby? I didn't send flowers— I knew you'd be deluged." She glanced around the room at the profusion of vases.

I couldn't wait to tell her how proud I was to have produced a healthy baby, how I used everything I learned in natural childbirth class—the abdominal breathing, the grunts, the pelvic tilts. I wanted to tell her how triumphant I felt when I defied my hateful obstetrician, a pint-sized sultan who warned me against nursing: "Your breasts will look like shrunken sacks!" He also told me that I was "showing off" choosing natural childbirth, but I knew better.

After my baby was born, he was whisked away by the nurse. I was left alone on the operating table in that icy room, staring into florescent lights overhead. What were they doing to him? I wanted to hold my baby and look at him. Suddenly I developed a blinding headache. I cried for help but no one came. Finally, they brought me to my room and told me they would bring my baby. But Mother's attention was diverted as she poked a finger into one of the vases to assess the water level.

"Dear, I'm going to ask the nurse for a pitcher so I can add some water. It's a shame to let these flowers die." And off she went.

Despite my yearning for my mother's approval, I never voiced my need to have her support. I wouldn't have known how to ask. Our family credo was: "Never look back. Don't dwell on something that you can't do anything about. Keep busy. Chin up, stomach in, shoulders back, feeling fit." This was what my mother chanted to us children on our Sunday walks.

By the time I was in my 40s, I realized how ill at ease I was with my mother. She was always so tense. I felt as if her bedroom was strung with high tension power lines. But I didn't know how to induce her to relax, to enjoy a laugh with me.

There were so many rules, most of them about clothes. "Don't wear purple—it makes you look sallow . . . Your hem should be one-quarter inch shorter in front . . . Wear white next to your face." Being a docile daughter, the last rule meant that I had a closet full of dresses and blouses with white Peter Pan collars. My husband, meanwhile, urged me to wear something sexy. "You have a great figure—show it off."

One day, after I came home from shopping with my mother, I timidly showed Hank a fashionable black silk cocktail dress with the ubiquitous Peter Pan collar. My normally good-natured husband exploded.

"Will you stop letting your mother choose your clothes?"

I finally gathered the nerve to decline my mother's shopping invitations and bought my first V-necked dress.

Mother may have been wrong about necklines but, observing her, I learned how to make friends. Walking into a party where I didn't know anyone never scared me, because I always say to the first person in my path, "Tell me a little about yourself. What interests you?" It's a sure way to engage a stranger in a meaningful conversation, and I learned about it from my mother.

Years ago, when I watched my mother profess interest in others, I was extremely cynical. "I'll bet she doesn't remember a word that person said," I grumbled. Maybe not, but I've had fascinating conversations that began with my tossing a question to a stranger. And by using my mother's technique, I rescued myself from feeling shy and ill at ease.

In 1960, I visited my parents in Honolulu. I was dismayed to find that their usual companionable relationship had turned frosty. When my father spoke to my mother, she invariably snapped, "I can't hear you, Arthur." Even though Mother had hearing loss, I suspected she exaggerated the problem to irritate her husband. Often at dinner, always at a restaurant, the two rarely spoke at all. My father looked off into the distance and occasionally wet his lips. Now and then my mother imparted some gossip to me, about her friends.

What had my father done wrong, I wondered, observing his contrite behavior. I thought of the pert blonde dancing teacher, Miss T., who, decades earlier, was his favorite exhibition partner on television. Could he have had an affair with her? Had Mother recently found out? In any case, Miss T. had died years ago, and it was time for forgiveness and reconciliation.

One afternoon, when my father was doing errands, I found Mother in her yellow and white bedroom slowly thumping the keys on her portable typewriter.

"Mother, could we talk?" I ventured.

She turned around. "What's on your mind, Baby?"

I swallowed nervously. "Mother, you and Daddy don't seem to be getting along. Has something happened?"

She glared at me, then thumped out her words as emphatically as she typed. "That is none of your goddamned business! Kindly keep your nose out of our affairs."

That was my last attempt to forge a close relationship with my mother. Shortly after that, she descended into dementia. Working on this book, I put off writing about her. Like a frustrated butterfly catcher, I couldn't pin her down. There were too many Kathryns: she was the life of the party and the charismatic performer, as well as the young mother whose flat voice expressed deepening depression.

I began to understand her when I read an article she wrote, "I was an Ugly Duckling." Kathryn, even as a grandmother, was an exceedingly pretty woman. But no amount of adulation from worshipful fans could erase my mother's image of herself as an "ugly runt." She drove herself unmercifully no matter what the task was. Even the twice-a-year ritual of organizing clothes closets had to be done so perfectly that the job left her with an aching back.

In dementia, though, she discovered a rare pleasure. Hour after hour, she watched tapes of *The Arthur Murray Party*. Did she recognize herself dancing, cavorting about, swinging from a chandelier? My only clue was that she never took her eyes away from the screen.

And now, there was no one to criticize her.

On my next trip to Honolulu, she didn't recognize me.

CHAPTER 17

My real mother

Helen reading to our son Peter.

Helen was cast out, a refugee from her own family. Our family not only wanted her, we needed her. Even when she was gone.

When I'm in the kitchen, Helen is always with me in spirit. She's there when I rub olive oil into the craggy recesses of my black iron skillet to keep it from rusting. Helen taught me how to soften a stale loaf of bread by sprinkling it with a few drops of water, then wrapping the loaf in foil and heating it. I have no doubt, as Helen told me, that cigar ashes will remove ring marks from a table. Alas, Grampe, who could have provided ashes from his fragrant-smelling cigars, is no longer with us.

Tonight, fixing the evening meal for my husband and me, I catch myself glancing up at the kitchen clock, as Helen used to do. She prepared dinner for my parents as if the meal were a production that necessitated an exact curtain time. Carrying a tray full of glasses, she wore the same purposeful frown. Her teeth were clamped on her lower lip until she made it safely to the counter.

After dinner, I spoon leftover rice or potatoes into one of Helen's Pyrex refrigerator dishes. The top fits perfectly. Lids on new models clamp with such ferocity I have to ask my husband to separate the two. I wash our plates and silverware by hand. Helen had no use for dishwashers. I can hear her voice as she wielded a sink brush, "How much time does it take to wash a few dishes?"

Father found her both plain and clumsy. So he gave her dancing lessons.

When I was a small child in our colonial style house in Harrison, New York, Helen's room was a haven for me. Actually it was two rooms. In her bedroom was her silver hand mirror and brush that she displayed on a crisp white doily on her bureau. The initials, intertwined like vines, had belonged to someone else. The sitting room—we called it her "little room"—was furnished with a couch and a radio, a proud RCA Victor model with a half-moon speaker. On the floor was a mound of multicolored strips of rags, the colors as brilliant as a kaleidoscope, that Helen used to make into hooked rugs.

Once a week, after supper, Phyllis and I sat on Helen's couch, Helen between us, listening to Major Bowes's *Original Amateur Hour*. I recall there was always a whistler, a woman who recited the poem "Trees," and a banjo player who sang "She'll be coming round the mountain." While the judges were conferring, we three solemnly debated the merits of the contestants.

When I was as old as 5 or 6, I often awakened to the pleasant warmth of wet sheets. I lay curled up until the warmth faded. Then shedding my wet gown, I ran shivering down the hall to Helen's room. Helen's face ordinarily registered fierce displeasure at any infraction of the rules—she liked to boast that we never played with our silverware or talked with our mouth full. But she never expressed annoyance at these awakenings. She bundled me into a bath towel and shooed me to my bedroom where she helped me pull on a clean gown. Sleepily, I watched her swiftly change my bed.

The story of how Helen came to live with my mother's family, the Kohnfelders, sounded like a fairy tale. When Helen's widowed father, a German immigrant, remarried, the new stepmother didn't want her. So, Helen, who was a rawboned, plain-looking 14-year-old, was cast out, like Hansel and Gretel. My grandmother, Lenore, whom we called "Nana," must have recognized that Helen would be a good worker, and gave her a home. The Kohnfelder family lived on two floors of a big two-family house in Jersey City. As the "hired girl," Helen washed and ironed and starched all the white shirts for the menfolk, including Abe; his father, Charles Sigmund; and son, Norman. Laundry was a grueling job that occupied an entire day every week.

As Helen once related, "I soaked clothes the night before in soapy water. Then I put them in the boiler. When they started to boil I'd poke them with a stick, then put them in the wash tub and scrub them on a washboard." Lastly, Helen opened the window and, with wooden clothespins, began the laborious job of hanging the wash on the line. The line was attached on either end to a pulley that was fastened to the building. To reach the garment required a sharp tug of the rope.

"Nana had me hang out nine-by-twelve rag rugs. It was a wonder the line didn't snap and fling me out the window," she said.

After Phyllis and I were born, Helen came to live with us. First, she was a nursemaid, then she became the cook. Helen ran a tight ship. Talking after bedtime brought a *thump, thump* of the broom handle on the kitchen ceiling. Continued giggling provoked threats, delivered in person, "to tan your bottom." No matter how irate Helen sounded, we knew she would be there the next morning to wake us up for school, her breath smelling deliciously of "caw-fee," as Helen pronounced it in her Jersey accent.

In those formal days of the 1930s, matrons dressed their maids in uniforms rarely seen today, except in a drawing room comedy. Bertha, our upstairs maid, a sweet-faced young woman from Ireland, most often wore a wine-colored cotton dress, stiff with starch, topped by a white collar. Her white organdy apron and a wisp of a white organdy cap were like doll's clothing. Bertha's replies to Mother's remarks were as proper as her uniform. "Yes, m'am, no m'am . . . " Helen had no use for such obsequious behavior. She was a member of the family. She had wiped little Kathryn's bottom, as she frequently reminded us. Consequently, she called my mother, her former charge, by her first name.

This familiarity could prove difficult for a young matron intent on running a model home. Inducing Helen to try a new dish required diplomacy. Cookbook in hand, Mother sat down across from Helen at the kitchen table. Helen was chopping celery in a wooden bowl, wielding the scythe-bladed tool with fierce intensity.

"Nothing is better than your roast chicken," Mother said smiling at Helen, but just for a change what did she think of this recipe? Frowning, Helen read the lengthy instructions for preparing coq au vin.

"Arthur won't like it," she said, resuming her chopping. "Too much fat."

Helen called my father by his first name but treated him with a trifle more deference. Since my father, as described by Helen, was "a fusspot," she enjoyed the challenge of pleasing him. "Your father ate good," she frequently related while tucking us in bed. It was a different story when my father complained about something. One Saturday morning, I was playing underneath the kitchen table, pretending it was a ship. Daddy walked in and told Helen that he didn't like the creases in the sleeves of his dress shirts—she should use a sleeve board. Then I heard the squeak of the kitchen door opening and closing and he left for the dancing studio.

Helen at the beach with Phyllis and me. No one could manage children like Helen. Even when they chose *not* to be managed, testing both propriety and the water.

I crawled out from under the table to look at Helen. My worst fears were justified. Her face looked as if it were carved of gray stone. I tiptoed out of the kitchen and ran up the stairs to our bedroom. "Phyllis," I cried, "Helen has on her mad face." We looked at each other helplessly, knowing what lay ahead. Helen refused to talk for two days, then mysteriously the storm clouds lifted, and Helen was sifting flour for her chocolate cake and telling us we could lick the bowl if we'd stop jiggling.

Although my father could be hurtful, it was he who changed Helen's life. As a girl, Helen was exceedingly clumsy. Grampe made jokes about her flat-footed walk. "She's as graceful as an elephant," he said. But, as families do, he accepted her clumsiness. Not Arthur. The first time Helen served dinner to my parents, he was appalled to see that a young woman, plain as she was, could be so awkward.

"She needs dancing lessons," he told my mother when Helen was back in the kitchen. Kathryn palled at the thought of persuading Helen to accept Arthur's generosity, but Arthur was equal to the task. Brooking no arguments, he made arrangements for Helen's first dancing lesson at the New York studio on the following Thursday. I can only imagine her teacher's initial trials, akin to breaking in a wild horse. But as my father had prophesied, after several hundred lessons, Helen emerged as a graceful dancer.

Thursdays, then widely reserved for "maid's day out," Helen would meet her friend, Ruth, a secretary from Flushing, Long Island. One morning, I had seen Helen's outfit, a navy blue suit and straw hat with a blue flower, neatly laid on her bed. Later, the two friends took a bus for lunch at the Automat, and then another bus to Arcadia Dance Hall. Arcadia was not as fancy as Roseland, Helen said, "but there's no drinking except beer and the men have nice manners."

Even as a teenager, I felt like Helen's little girl. She was a great loving feature in our lives. From left, Phyllis, Helen Edelbach, and Jane.

The next morning, when Helen awakened us, traces of pink lipstick still on her upper lip, we plied her with questions about her partners. "Was Ray Hill there?" I asked.

"Oh, sure," Helen replied with a satisfied smile."

I felt a flutter of fear in my stomach. I didn't want Helen to marry Ray Hill and leave us. One Friday morning, a week later, Helen's blue eyes were unusually bright. "Ray Hill and I won the waltz contest," she said. We begged for details. "I wasn't planning on going in. But Ray came over and said, 'Let's give it a try.' Ruth egged me on. We started waltzing. The judges walked around the dance floor tapping other couples on the shoulder to sit down. I was sure one was heading for us." She shook her head at our questions.

"Pretty soon they turned the spotlight on us. I don't know how long we danced. You should have heard the applause when they announced we were the winners. They gave us a beautiful silver cup. Ray wanted me to have it.

"No, girls, it's getting late. I'll show you the cup when you get home from school."

When Helen died in her early 90s, I found the tarnished cup among the knick-knacks on her shelf. The eight-inch cup was engraved *Arcadia Ball Room Waltz Contest Winner 1934*. Tears came to my eyes. The cup looked so small.

My childhood fear that Helen would marry and leave us proved to be unfounded. In a sense, Helen was married to my family. To my knowledge, we only failed her once.

This occurred when my father moved us to Beverly Hills. We left more than our house and books. We left Helen, whose home had been "the little room" ever since we were born. With my mother's help, Helen moved to New York and rented an apartment on First Avenue.

During our one and a half years in movieland, Mother wrote frequently to Helen and reminded us to do so. But postcards and photos couldn't disguise the fact that Helen was no longer needed by my family. When we returned to New York from Hollywood, Mother found Helen mumbling with depression and suffering from painful shingles.

My father, not burdened by my mother's paralyzing guilt, quickly arrived at a solution. He put Helen in charge of the cleaning staff at the dancing studio. When I took a dancing lesson or, years later, briefly worked as a teacher, I'd catch a glimpse of Helen in her smock, a dust rag emerging from one of the wide pockets. I'd wave to her—she'd wave back, but I could tell from her purposeful walk that she felt there was work to be done.

When Philip, the firstborn of our four, came into the world, he was treated like one of Helen's own. As a small child, when he came down with chicken pox, whooping cough, or measles, I would immediately call Helen and ask for her help. The answer was always yes, despite the fact that Helen lived in a third-floor walk-up apartment on First Avenue in New York City, and we lived in Rye, a fifty-minute train ride from Grand Central Station.

Several hours later, having navigated city bus, commuter train, and suburban taxi, she appeared like Mary Poppins on our doorstep. Quickly removing her straw hat or wool headgear, depending on the season, Helen marched briskly into Philip's room, her jutting jaw reflecting her determination to do battle with illness.

Except for forays into kitchen and laundry room to get things cleaned up, Helen kept Philip company through his illness while he showed her his baseball collection, or she read to him or sat contentedly in a chair while he slept.

Even after my own children were born, I remained as dependent on Helen as I had been as a child. At this time I was writing a column for an out-of-town newspaper. Instead of using teenage babysitters, I got in the habit of calling Helen to "spend a day or two" at the house. Soon, Helen was spending most of her time with us.

Having such a close relationship with my childhood nurse had its drawbacks. As time went on, I resented Helen's mothering, so much more successful than my own. Philip's younger brother, Peter, a self-sufficient child, tolerated Helen's disciplinary ways, but his younger twin sisters complained that she was too strict. Helen, stolid and determined, muttered that "those girls needed breaking in." Tensions came to a head when Hank and I traveled to Europe to attend a medical meeting.

Fearful at putting Helen in sole charge of my rebellious crew, I engaged a housekeeper, whom Helen would relieve at certain times. We returned to see Helen seated ramrod stiff in the living room, glowering. "Your housekeeper turned out to be a drunk," she said, and spat out an account of "a wild party right in your own house." Eventually, the hurts were mended and we wordlessly resumed our easy, loving relationship.

In 1969, when Hank accepted a position as director of surgery at The Jewish Hospital in Cincinnati, we pulled up stakes. After much coaxing, we persuaded Helen—then in her 80s—to move to our adopted city. I suspect one of the appeals was that Philip, a bachelor, lived in Cincinnati.

The first apartment I chose for Helen had a small backyard; it was so quiet you could hear bird sounds. Helen flatly turned it down, saying that she liked having something to look at. My husband's "find"—an apartment on a busy street—met with her approval.

Helen's apartment once again became a haven for me. Whenever I had the urge to see her or needed a captive audience to rehearse a speech, I stopped by. I stood outside her four-unit apartment building and rang the bell. The maple tree across the street, pure flame in the fall, was reflected in the glass door.

Within a minute or two, Helen's shapely bluish-veined legs, her feet in chenille bedroom slippers, came into view descending the stairs. Following her into her apartment, I sniffed the warm aroma of pea soup or applesauce or freshly baked granola cookies that she obligingly made to comply with my new holistic health ideas. On a cooking day, Helen wore a smock and a hair net. Her small kitchen housed a vast collection of jars and plastic containers that she had saved as take-outs for Philip or me.

At some point, I always asked her, "What are you having for dinner?"

"I'm having a pork chop," she said one afternoon, her eyes sparkling in anticipation. "I got a lovely meaty one at Kroger—and I'm fixing some red cabbage and string beans." The dinette table was already set for dinner, covered with one of her cross-stitched tablecloths, a matching cloth napkin and a jelly jar for drinking.

When I asked, "How was your day?" Helen had a ready answer.

"I washed the windows from the inside. I used to do the outside but I let them do it," she'd say, as if tossing the window cleaners a bone.

On one of my visits, I asked Helen about her childhood. I knew she had a German-born father and an older sister, Emma, but I learned little else about her. I wasn't prepared for the anger and bitterness that distorted her face. "We weren't allowed on the street," she said. "When people talked to us, we'd start to cry. We had to be so quiet at the table. There was no fun in that house."

I thought of our Christmas mornings as children. When we rushed down the stairs eager to dig into our mound of toys, Helen was always there, sitting by the tree, a look of anticipation on her face.

Now and then, Philip's visit coincided with mine. "Helen, could you sew on this button . . . " Peering into a pot or sampling a cookie, his face reflected the ready happiness of the much-loved child, confident that he was bestowing joy by his presence. I felt a pang at his basking in her love, which we have learned to call "unconditional." As a young mother, mine was doled out mostly as a reward.

Take-outs in hand, a peck on Helen's cheek, Philip and I clomped down the stairs. Outside, we stopped for a final glimpse of Helen at the window, waving goodbye to two of her children.

In the spring of 1982, when I visited Helen at her apartment, I noticed that her voice was slightly slurred. "That's nothing," Helen said. "I'm not going to give a speech." But when the slurring became more pronounced, I encouraged her to see a speech therapist. Shortly after, I received a letter from Dr. Wood: *Helen Edelbach's symptoms in most cases are suggestive of Amyotrophic Lateral Sclerosis.* The doctor recommended that I consult a neurologist. My heart sank. I phoned the office of the director of neurology, Dr. Frederick Samaha, and was able to make an appointment within a few weeks.

Helen and I sat in the waiting room making small talk. "Asparagus is still very high," she said, "39 cents a bunch." She shook her head. "I can wait. I don't pay those prices."

Dr. Samaha, his warm brown eyes putting us at ease, shook hands with Helen and invited me to join them in his office. Yes, she was having a little trouble chewing her food. How did he know that? She hadn't told me about the food. "I won't starve," Helen said with a lopsided smile. "I mash up my food in a blender."

More questions, an occasional bravado answer from Helen that evoked a smile from the doctor. *He treats her like a queen*, I thought, close to tears. The interview over, the doctor said gently, "Helen, you have a condition called ALS. It's better known as Lou Gehrig's disease." He patted her hand. "I want to see you in two weeks."

Helen continued preparing her food in the blender. But the disease refused to stay still. Soon Helen became too weak to bathe or dress herself. I quickly formed a nursing squad consisting of our cleaning woman, Lena; housekeeper, Maude; and when needed, Maude's daughter, Winnie.

I stopped in Helen's apartment every day to check on their activities. Like a nursing superintendent, I discussed the patient's condition with each caregiver and distributed pay checks. On one visit, out of the corner of my eye, I could see Helen seated on the couch staring at the opposite wall. I quickly took out my list—Vaseline for Helen's chapped lips, disposable briefs. *Better hurry before the drugstore closes.*

The next week I gathered a batch of photos to show Helen. They were mostly of Philip—his new apartment, posing with Helen, sampling her soup. When I came in, Helen was sitting on the couch. "Look, Hely, I've got some pictures to show you." I handed her a photo. She took it, but put it down without looking at it. My eyes pricked with tears. *I've lost Helen*, I thought. Driving home, I couldn't stop crying.

That same week, Hank received an invitation to attend a meeting of chest surgeons in Sweden. I told Hank that I couldn't leave now.

"You'd only be gone ten days," Hank protested. "She won't know whether you're here or not." A pause. "You know how great those international meetings are."

I gave in, and ten days later we flew to Stockholm. As Hank had predicted, there were gala events every night. Lavish buffets where Hank and I headed for the platters of delicately flavored pink smoked salmon. Women, particularly those from Latin America, sparkled in ballgowns and jewels. I hardly thought about Helen until Philip called the day before we were to leave for home.

"I'm sorry, Mom, Helen died last night."

I felt as wooden as Helen had looked staring at the wall. *I shouldn't have gone*, I thought, squeezing my eyes shut. *I shouldn't have gone.*

After she died, I began to understand my behavior during Helen's illness. I couldn't face her death. So instead of sitting on the couch with her, holding her hand, or acting as one of her caregivers, I kept the pain at bay doing errands and organizing schedules.

For years after her death, I dreamed about Helen. In one recurrent dream I saw her wearing her navy blue coat and straw hat, dining at an outdoor restaurant. Another time, I suddenly realized I hadn't talked to her for months and frantically flipped through my telephone book for the number. She was sitting on a park bench, or boarding the Lexington Avenue bus. Always out of reach.

Helen's story was one of a life filled with her special brand of tough love. It was also the story of my real mother.

CHAPTER 18

Midlife crisis

Discovering holistic health, a new world opened.

Just when things

seemed most bleak,

I discovered an entire

field of healing largely

unnoticed by mainstream

America. A new

world opened for me.

It was the spring of 1971, and I wasn't sure whether our marriage would survive. The children, Philip and Peter, 18 and 19, and the twins, 11, were subdued and watchful. It never occurred to me to provide psychological counseling for them anymore than I considered seeking such help for myself.

My life is falling apart, I thought, forcing myself to get dressed to go to a dinner party at a friend's house. For five years, I had written a decorating column. I was bored with writing about skylights and couches. Nothing gripped me.

My personal life was as uninspired as my writing. At the end of a walk, a friend looked quizzically at me. "I do all the talking. You haven't said a word about yourself." The truth was that I didn't trust anyone enough to talk about my feelings. Most disturbing, I never felt completely well. I had frequent sore throats and chest colds. Added to that, I had trouble sleeping. It never occurred to me that I could treat these minor problems myself. Instead, for every little ailment, I went running to my doctor.

At the dinner party later that evening, a chance remark led me on a path that I could never have imagined.

At dinner, the man on my left asked me if I had heard about a new medical center called the Psi Center in Greenhills, a suburb of Cincinnati. Later I learned that Psi stands for physical, spiritual, and intellectual. "They're doing some kookie things out there," he said.

"Kookie" caught my attention. As a newspaper writer, I was always on the lookout for an off-beat subject. The next morning I called the Psi Center and made an appointment to visit later that week.

Take charge. Be self-reliant. The patient actually has a say. What a radical notion.

As I waited for Dr. Robert Zieve in the homey waiting room, sunlight streamed through the large window. On one table was a profusion of plants. I recognized grape ivy and aloe. It looked like any old-fashioned doctor's office until I took a closer look at the books displayed on another table. One was *Occult Medicine Can Save Your Life*, by C. Norman Shealy; another, *The Edgar Cayce Handbook for Health through Drugless Therapy*. Those were curious titles, I thought.

I picked up a brochure about the Psi Center—*a center for the alignment of body, mind and spirit*—and read a few paragraphs. Why was a medical center messing around with mind and spirit? Was this Christian Science?

In time, I learned that Dr. Zieve was a pioneer in the field of integrative medicine, and he was directing his holistic medical clinic long before such work was popular.

When he breezed into the waiting room, he had brown curly hair, a beard, and was dressed in a purple-figured shirt. "I'm not against orthodox medicine," he said, "but I believe that other methods must be integrated." Dr. Zieve led me into his small examining room where he began to describe foot reflexology, one of the alternative therapies he was using.

"Certain reflex areas on the bottom and sides of the feet correspond to various organs of the body," he said, pointing to diagrammed drawings of the right and left foot and proceeding to identify each specific area. The big toe was labeled "pituitary." On the left foot was an area that corresponded to the heart; its mirror image on the right foot was "gall bladder."

As Dr. Zieve described how reflexology had benefitted a patient suffering from colitis, I began to experience a sinking feeling that is familiar to writers: *what is this man talking about and how am I ever going to explain it?* I was relieved when Dr. Zieve looked at his watch and said that Dr. Robert Rothan, a dentist on the staff, would discuss nutrition with me. That subject promised to make some sense.

I was in for some surprises.

Dr. Rothan, tall and lanky, spoke at a breakneck pace. "Balance is the name of the game. Nutrition is a tool to help you find balance. Low blood sugar, fatigue, depression"—in the outpouring of words I caught *alcoholism, stroke, kidney stones, schizophrenia*—"are related to an inability to handle carbohydrates."

"Think in terms of your automobile. We put in processed white sugar—the blood sugar shoots up. When the blood sugar drops, we're tired, depressed. Sodium potassium imbalance, magnesium deficiency, carbohydrate metabolism defect . . ."

I listened dazed to the damage caused by processed foods, then snapped to attention when Dr. Rothan said, "That's the beauty of our testing method. When you learn to listen to your body, you get definite instructions."

From a jar that he identified as magnesium, he took a capsule and said, "Now hold this in your left hand. Straighten your right arm—hold it stiff; keep the hand on a level with your head. Now when I press down, resist with your full strength."

He looked at the opposite wall and chanted, "Will magnesium benefit this body? If yes, make her strong; if no, make her weak."

Using two fingers, Rothan pressed down on my wrist. I tensed my arm as hard as I could, but he pushed it down easily.

"You don't need magnesium."

Going to the shelf, he placed another capsule in my left hand. "Now be as strong as you can. Will this body benefit from Vitamin E? If yes, make her strong. If no, make her weak."

Again, I exerted all my strength to withstand the pressure on my wrist, but my arm sank down weakly.

"Let's try some iron."

Memory flicked back to a bout of anemia as a young woman. I remembered horse-sized capsules, a metallic taste.

"Will iron benefit this body?" Dr. Rothan chanted.

Again, I tensed my arm while he pressed down on my wrist, a throbbing vessel in his forehead attesting to the exertion, but this time, to my surprise, I was able to raise his arm.

"Maybe you knew that I needed iron and you didn't press as hard," I ventured.

"It's not necessary for me to know what we're testing for," Rothan said. "You can write the word on a piece of paper and hold it in your hand, or simply keep the thought in your mind."

I couldn't deny that my testing arm was weak at times, strong at other times depending on the substance being tested. But how did this voodoo testing work?

"We are speaking to the consciousness of your body," Dr. Rothan said. "You and your body are nothing more than a projection of energy." I felt like Alice in Wonderland talking to the Mad Hatter.

Driving home, I puzzled over the mysterious arm-testing whose proper name is kineseology. I considered arm-testing certain foods with a friend but was afraid that it wouldn't work and I would feel foolish. "You have to believe in the process," Dr. Rothan had said.

I talked to several dental colleagues of Dr. Rothan who had witnessed his demonstration of muscle-testing. They were as flabbergasted as I was by the experience.

But I couldn't let go of the subject. The day after my visit to the Psi Center I drove to Cincinnati's downtown public library. Poring over the *Readers' Guide* (this was

My book was translated into half a dozen languages and sold all over the world. It was my turn in the spotlight, and I enjoyed every minute of it.

well before the Internet), I was amazed to find that healing centers, similar to the Psi Center, were springing up like mushrooms all over the country. It was uncanny that, in many instances, one center—say the Holistic Heath Center in San Diego—had no contact with the Institute for the New Age of Man in New York City, and yet the language employed by these two centers was remarkably alike.

Each talked about a new definition of health. Health is body, mind and spirit. If you regularly lose your temper, you're not well.

The battle cry of all the centers I learned about was self-reliance. "Take charge of your health! No one knows your body as well as you."

The doctor-patient relationship had undergone a sea change. The patient was no longer unquestionably obedient. "Yes, Doc, no, Doc, anything you say, Doc." Instead, the patient was in charge and simply used the doctor as a resource.

Breathing in the dry library air, I felt my heart racing. *Jane, you're onto something,* I whispered. I felt as if I were in a bobsled poised at the top of a run.

I was so captivated by holistic health that when I heard about "The Healing Conference of the Future" in San Diego in the fall of 1976, I was determined to be there. After the conference, I planned to spend a week at Meadowlark, a holistic live-in retreat in Hemet, California, modeled after European spas such as the Bircher-Benner Clinic in Zurich. I, who had never gone anywhere without my husband, made plane and hotel reservations for myself, feeling as if it were a great accomplishment. With a tingle of excitement and nervousness, I packed my suitcase and groaned when I tried lifting it. Traveling with Hank, I had never realized how heavy a suitcase was in the days before rollers.

I have a habit of skimming over factual data, which is what I did with the conference material. I thought I had read that the meeting began Thursday evening at 8:30. That evening, with an hour to spare, my taxi from the airport pulled up to the venerable El Cortez hotel in San Diego. An elderly bellman took my suitcase.

I was surprised there were so few people in the lobby. Standing by the front desk, I asked the bellman where the holistic conference was taking place. Scanning his written material he told me that the welcome ceremony was scheduled for the Don room at 7:30 the next night.

"No," I said patiently, "the conference starts this evening."

"No, ma'am," the bellman said. "Tomorrow night." The clerk at the front desk settled the argument: the conference started the following night.

When I realized I had read the crucial information mistakenly, I was close to tears. It had been such a rush to get ready, to organize the childrens' meals and activities during my absence. Here I was alone in San Diego. What would I do with myself? I didn't know anyone. While the bellman waited patiently with my suitcase, the desk clerk tapped the check-in form.

"We have you down for a standard single, but I could let you have the studio suite on the top floor for the same price. The couch makes into a bed—you'll be very comfortable."

"I'll look at it," I said bleakly. The bellman and I rode silently to the penthouse floor in the hotel's much acclaimed, glass enclosed elevator.

With clanging of keys, he opened the door and switched on a dim ceiling light. I glimpsed windows on each wall hung with white voile curtains. The bellman, with some effort, opened the windows and, one by one, the curtains began a wild flapping. I ran to the window overlooking the entire landscape of the San Diego bay, Coronado, the city—and breathed in the salt air of the Pacific Ocean. The neon letters on the rooftop that spelled El Cortez cast a rosy light on my window sill.

After the bellman left, I surveyed my enchanted room. *This is mine for a precious day,* I exulted, looking out another window. I would venture out tomorrow and explore the waterfront, knowing my rooftop home was waiting for me.

The conference took place in the convention center adjacent to the hotel. No need to have brought my best tailored suit; a great many attendees were dressed in loose gauze outfits and sandals.

The conference was a crazy wonderful three-ring circus. Dr. C. Norman Shealy described his holistic techniques to alleviate pain. Olga Worrall, in her tiny veiled hat and fur stole, looked more like a club woman than a psychic healer. Dr. Carl Simonton claimed that visualization could strengthen the cancer patient's immune system. "Imagine that your white cells are ferocious dogs gobbling up your cancer cells," he said.

I, who barely passed algebra, was fascinated by physicist Fritjof Capra comparing new physics to Buddhist philosophy. "Sitting by the ocean one late summer afternoon, watching the waves . . . I felt its rhythm and I heard its sound, and at that moment I knew this was the Dance of Shiva . . . ."

Elisabeth Kubler Ross, whose book, *On Death and Dying,* had only recently been published, sat on the edge of the stage like Judy Garland. "Don't fear death," she said. "Death is like shedding a worn winter coat." I was touched by her remarks about love. "The ultimate lesson all of us have to learn is unconditional love, which includes not only others but ourselves as well."

When she had finished we stood up and clapped until our hands tingled. It was a groundswell, with everyone in that convention hall hugging one another. I had always greeted people with a firm handshake. A hug felt good.

I made my reservation at Meadowlark intending to do an article about America's first holistic line-in retreat for a Cincinnati newspaper, and Dr. Evarts G. Loomis, its founder, offered to have me accompany him on the hour-and-a-half drive from San Diego to Hemet, California. Knowing Dr. Loomis's exalted reputation as the "Father of Holistic Health," I called him Dr. Loomis, but he corrected me saying, "We only use first names at Meadowlark."

It was dark when we arrived at Meadowlark, too dark to see Tahquitz peak looming over the twenty-acre estate that had once belonged to movie mogul Louis B. Mayer. Evarts located my white stucco cottage and brought in my suitcase. He hugged me, stiffly.

"That's what we do at Meadowlark, " he explained, and left with a wave of his hand.

I poked around my cottage, sparse but inviting, and found a small "welcome" basket with several slices of banana bread and apples. Another surprise: I looked out the window and saw a grapefruit tree growing in the front yard. I walked outside and under a canopy of stars picked a chubby little ball. I peeled the thick skin and popped a section of fruit in my mouth. It was slightly sour but chewy and satisfying.

The next morning I awakened in the clear desert air to a colorful world of purple bougainvillea, white oleander, eucalyptus, glossy grape vines.

But I didn't spend too much time gazing at flowers and trees. The night before, I had asked Evarts if there was a jogging track and he had pointed out where it was. I wanted to be sure I had my usual exercise routine.

After a three mile jog in the cool morning air, I headed for the nearby chapel. Inside, an ecumenical display of religious symbols—Jesus, Buddha, Moses, and others—and a pleasing smell of cedar. A thin young man, eyes closed, sat cross-legged on a mat, facing me. I closed my eyes for a few minutes, but remembering that breakfast was at 8, I checked my watch and jumped to my feet.

When I arrived at the dining room, I stood with others around the circular wood tables. Evarts asked us to join hands and said a short prayer. I felt a little awkward holding a stranger's hands—should I give a parting squeeze? The prayer over, I helped myself to the appetizing items on the lazy Susan in the center of the table, including granola, steaming millet cereal, a pitcher of nut milk, blueberry muffins. To my surprise, I was the only guest in jogging shorts. Several had canes, one parked a walker within easy reach. Later, notebook in hand, I bustled about interviewing guests. So many guests were plagued with arthritis and other ills that I felt as if I was the only healthy person present.

My first inkling that I was not as healthy as I had thought occurred in art class.

We sat at a table with a box of pastels. "I'm going to play music," our teacher Mary Jean said. "Close your eyes and let the feelings flow out of your hand onto the paper." I looked around at my classmates. Pam, a librarian, was covering the paper with Chagall-like colors. Jim, a pilot, was bent over a drawing, totally absorbed. I took a deep breath, drew a stick figure trying to climb a mountain. It was a cramped, shaky little drawing covering a small portion of the paper. Worse, one by one, members of the class showed their drawings and described them fluently. When my turn came, I asked to be excused.

"We're not going to force you but sharing can be helpful," Mary Jean said kindly. I finally agreed and listened miserably to the comments.

Later, Pam asked, "How are you feeling? I'm so glad you shared your drawing." I tried to manage a smile, but I did no better with clay. "Close your eyes, create what you would like to become," Mary Jean suggested. My classmates produced what I thought were abstract marvels of expression.

I patted out the same ashtray I had learned to make in kindergarten.

A breakthrough in getting in touch with my feelings came during the Intensive Journal Workshop of Ira Progoff. Our teacher asked us to write about a meaningful episode in our lives. I sat frozen, my mind blank, while others wrote intently. Finally, I forced myself to describe a painful incident that had occurred some months earlier. My husband and I were at a dance. I was jitterbugging with a gay young man. Bored, he spun me out and drew me in like a toy top.

While engaged in these gyrations, I could see my husband dancing with a pretty blonde woman, holding her very close. The music seemed to go on endlessly. Now, pencil in hand, picturing the comfortable way they fitted into one another's arms, I wondered if they were lovers.

After a half hour, we read our writing aloud. Ruth, an obese schoolteacher dressed in a caftan, recalled swimming with her beloved father, hanging on to his chest hair to keep up with him. Sharon described her feelings the evening her former husband asked her for a divorce.

When it was my turn, I struggled to keep my voice steady, and felt relieved when I had finished. Ruth swooped over to me, engulfed me in an embrace. "I know what an effort that cost you," she said. "I could see the muscle twitching in your cheek."

That was my first awareness that it's okay to reveal your feelings and to show your pain. Back home, the thawing process continued. I learned to voice my feelings more honestly with friends, which gave them the opportunity to do the same. Instead of my customary firm handshake—keeping people at arm's length—I hugged people, even new acquaintances.

Marital hurts heal slowly, but eventually I was able to see my husband as a person struggling with his own fears and frustrations.

At some point, being a spectator of the holistic movement was not enough. I wanted to be a recognized participant, to make my mark as a writer, to bring this message of good health to others.

I knew I wanted to start with the little known subject of homeopathy. I was introduced to this system of medicine one evening at Meadowlark when Evarts talked about his daughter who lived in the wilds of Montana.

"She has no doctors nearby so she depends on her homeopathic kit to treat herself and her family."

That struck a nerve. Being able to treat your own everyday ailments without running to the doctor for every little thing was appealing to me. I soon learned that homeopathic remedies had been used the world over for more than 200 years. The Royal family in Great Britain were homeopathic patients. Homeopathy was immensely popular in this country in the latter half of the 19th century. But at this time, the 1970s, only a small group of Americans had heard of homeopathy.

I resolved that I was going to change that.

CHAPTER 19

Resistance from the old guard

There was a missionary fervor to that early work.

Though little-known, there were still homeopathic schools and hospitals in America. But there wasn't a book I wanted to change that.

After I got home from Meadowlark, the idea of writing a book about homeopathy lingered in my mind. I thought about Evarts's daughter who lived in the wilds of Montana and cared for herself and her family with homeopathic remedies. I could be self-sufficient myself if I knew more about homeopathy. There were a great many books about the subject, but most were published in Great Britain and written in a flowery style that made me want to grab a red pencil.

What was needed was a how-to book about homeopathy that would tell ordinary people how to treat everyday ailments with homeopathic remedies. I felt sure I was the one to write this book.

Since I knew very little about my subject, I lugged faded cloth books about homeopathy, many with loose pages, home from the library. To my surprise, I learned that in the latter part of the 19th century there were twenty-two homeopathic medical schools and over a hundred homeopathic hospitals. Intellectuals such as Louisa May Alcott patronized homeopathic physicians. I remembered reading about Marmee in *Little Women* who dispensed belladonna, a homeopathic remedy, to neighbors stricken with scarlet fever. Sadly, belladonna wasn't able to cure Beth, one of the *Little Women*, whose death I imagine still provokes tears from young readers.

At first, the original family doctor scoffed. In time, even he became a convert.

The National Center for Homeopathy provided me with a Homeopathic Home Remedy kit, and with it I could familiarize myself with its remedies. The kit, a snug three-by-six-inch gray plastic box with a snap lock, contained twenty-eight of the most commonly used remedies. Doses came in tablet form; each vial, clearly labeled, contained 125 tablets.

Armed with my home remedy kit, which inspired the same affection in me as my first lunchbox, I could treat my minor ailments and injuries and minister to my family. I felt like the colonial dame dispensing herbs or the frontier woman with her doctor book.

When I became interested in homeopathy, our teenage son, Phil, liked to quip, "My mom is into nuts and berries." It wasn't long before Phil was a convert. I gave him aconite, a remedy to treat early symptoms of a cold, and allium cepa for a runny nose. After he had tried these, he stopped using over-the-counter cold medicines. Later, he learned to prescribe other homeopathic remedies for himself.

My reputation as a family dispenser of remedies was secured after I tried arnica. Made from a mountain flower, leopard's bane, arnica could be a lifesaver if an accident were to occur. That's why most homeopaths carry arnica with them.

I saw how well arnica works when I visited my sister, Phyllis. She had been standing on the top of the stairs, lost her balance, and fell down several steps. She wasn't seriously hurt though she looked dazed. I ran for my vial of arnica and dropped a few tablets in her mouth. Within minutes, the tablets dissolved and she recovered from shock. Later, Phyllis related that her bruises healed more quickly than usual.

At first, my husband scoffed at this "pseudoscience," which is what he was taught to call homeopathy in medical school. But his skepticism was short-lived. On our annual ski trip, I packed my arnica and took a preventive dose before I hit the slopes. Hank observed that I didn't complain about muscle strains or leg cramps and asked me if he could borrow my arnica.

At this time, the mid-1970s, proponents of holistic health were discovering homeopathy. Despite homeopathy being 200 years old, the relationship between the two was a natural marriage. Both systems advocated a "take charge of your health" message and were wary of the current practice of treating patients with powerful prescriptions and over-the-counter drugs. All the information strengthened my conviction that homeopathy's time had come.

But homeopathy was only a private passion until Shari Lewis breezed into town. Shari was a popular television ventriloquist with a beguiling puppet named Lamb Chop. She was in Cincinnati to promote her new children's show. I had met Shari when she appeared on my parents' television show. Now, as a hospitable gesture, I invited her to lunch.

Awaiting our soufflé at the Maisonette, then one of Cincinnati's outstanding restaurants, I talked nonstop about homeopathy. "Homeopathy is fascinating," I said to Shari. "No one knows how it works but the correct homeopathic remedy can overcome mental as well as physical problems. It's even safe for babies and children." I took out a vial of tiny white tablets from my purse. "A baby could swallow the contents of this entire vial and have no ill effects."

After launching into the benefits of homeopathy, I noticed that Shari had taken out her notebook and was scribbling furiously. "Jeremy will be fascinated by this," she said, continuing to write.

I caught my breath. Her husband, Jeremy, was a publisher, founder, and president of J.P. Tarcher, a publishing company that specialized in avant-garde medical subjects. The minute Shari told him about homeopathy, I knew he'd be on the phone assigning the subject to one of his writers.

"I'm planning to write Jeremy," I said and took a sip of water. "I'm sending him a book proposal."

When I got home, I composed my query letter to Jeremy. It was a letter that later caused me to howl with laughter. "This movement is cresting like a tidal wave," I wrote, "and I think we should jump on our surfboards!"

When I followed up with a phone call, Jeremy was enthusiastic but made one stipulation: "You must have an M.D. co-author." A pause. I had envisioned interviewing a number of homeopathic physicians, in journalistic fashion, but Jeremy was unbending. "With a little-known subject like homeopathy, you need a medical authority."

I set out like Prince Charming, in search of the homeopathic Cinderella. I traveled as far as San Francisco to find a doctor with an interest in self-help homeopathic medicine. No one fit the bill until I met Maesimund B. Panos, M.D. "Maisie", as everyone called her. Her father and late husband had been homeopaths, and she had founded a patients' group for those who wanted to learn more about this system of medicine. Another plus was that Maisie lived in Tipp City, a farm community only a little over an hour's drive from Cincinnati.

There was only one hitch: Maisie was not interested in co-authoring a book on homeopathy. On one of my visits to Tipp City to plead my case, she said, "I'm much too busy to write a book."

I hung on with the tenacity that sprang from desperation. Could she spare one day a month? Perhaps her secretary could gather some of her articles for me?

Finally I wore her down. "We could give it a try," she said, sighing deeply. We made a date to meet three weeks later for our first session.

On the appointed day, I arrived at 8 a.m. at the Panos' converted farmhouse and clomped up the wood stairs to Maisie's office. The door was open; I stood in front of her desk with an expectant smile. Maisie, in what show biz folk would call a "slow take," raised her eyes and looked at me as if trying to recall who I was.

"Did you receive my chapters?" I asked eagerly.

Maisie frowned. "I put them somewhere." She shuffled through stacks of correspondence and articles but my chapters never surfaced. During our morning session the phone rang constantly. Dr. Panos always answered on the first ring.

"My writer is here," Maisie said to a colleague on the phone. "We're working on our little book," she added, with an air of amusement.

Thus began a relationship that spelled misery for me. A wonderfully wise friend, whom I had known for years, deserved a medal for her patience during those three years when I was working on the book. I couldn't stop babbling about Dr. Panos. I was like a woman going through a divorce who can talk about nothing but her ex-spouse's behavior.

"I worked all week on this miserable chapter. Maisie's only comment was that she heartily disliked the journalistic style of addressing the reader as 'you.' You should read her writing. All passive verbs. 'It is to be surmised,' I groaned. I'm trying to make this lady sound like a warm, caring family doctor and she uses words that sound so pretentious . . ."

My voice trailed off. My friend looked at me. "Have you ever told Dr. Panos how her behavior makes you feel?" I was dumbfounded at the suggestion. I was brought up on Dale Carnegie, the best-selling sage who taught his disciples "how to win friends and influence people." I was taught not to confront but to compliment people.

Besides my faithful friend, I had another supportive person in my life, my editor, Janice Gallagher. In those days before e-mail, chapters flew back and forth like homing pigeons. I mailed my manuscript to Janice, who promptly returned the pages, their borders covered with tiny but legible writing. "Please differentiate homeopathy from herbalism. Describe more fully . . . Don't we need a comparison chart?"

To lighten the load, Janice seized upon every opportunity to include a pun. "Where is the pets chapter?" she asked. "I will dog your footsteps until I get it." Another: "Enclosed is your description of dental problems. This was a section I could really get my teeth into."

After three years of once-a-month meetings with Dr. Panos, I felt as if I knew every pothole in Interstate 75. When I passed the traffic sign to 275 west, I was fifteen minutes from home. Pulling up in our driveway, I opened the car door and, stiff from driving, hobbled up the back steps like a bowlegged cowboy. Opening the door, I went straight to the phone and called Janice. When she answered, I blurted, "I don't think I can work with her . . ."

Janice's voice was soothing. "You're doing so well," she said. "Those last few chapters work very well." I closed my eyes and let her words drip over me like warm oil.

One sunny November day, I had my last session with Maisie. We talked pleasantries while I gathered up my notebooks and ballpoint pens and clomped down the stairs for the last time. Heading south on I-75, I passed the familiar landmarks. I rolled down the window and opened the sunroof. I felt bathed in sunshine. I sang in my best musical comedy style, "I think you've done it. I think you've done it. I think-a-think-a-think . . . . "

Once *Homeopathic Medicine at Home* was on bookstore shelves, I wanted to introduce it to the homeopathic community. First, I wrote to the chairman of an upcoming conference in Philadelphia asking if I might attend and say a few words about the book. I felt sure this group would be elated to learn that a book about their beloved system of medicine was available. Homeopathy was little-known in this country at the time. The organization sent me a printed notice about the homeopathic meeting.

Opening day of the conference an audience of several hundred homeopathic physicians gathered to hear scientific papers. I wore my power red suit, which stood out nicely in a room of Puritan gray. Just before intermission, the chairman announced my name. Taking a deep breath, I walked to the microphone and told the audience what I felt certain would be welcome news: "Our publisher believes in publicizing this valuable system of medicine." I hinted at forthcoming television shows and newspaper stories.

When I was finished, I smiled at the audience and walked to my seat. There was scarcely a sound—no applause, not even a thank you. I tried to look unconcerned, but I was close to tears. Why was everyone so cool to me?

During the afternoon session, I sat next to a woman who looked friendly. I summoned nerve enough to question her. "I know that homeopathic remedies have been dispensed by a dozen or more homeopathic pharmacies for over a hundred years. What do you think about plans to introduce homeopathy at big chain drug stores?"

She smiled politely and shook her head. *We like it just as it is.* That was the last homeopathic conference I attended.

When *Homeopathic Medicine at Home* appeared in print four years after my lunch date with Shari, a much published friend warned me that the job was not finished. "You need to spend as much time promoting your book as you spent writing it."

This was the golden age of publishing, when publishers allocated money to promote a book and sent their authors on book tours. The logical person to publicize our book was its medical authority, Dr. Panos, but she considered such activities unsuitable for a doctor. Therefore, it was my job to represent the book and be present at all appearances and book signings.

But, first, thanks to my husband, I was slated to appear on *The Bob Braun Show,* then the top-rated live television program in the Midwest.

Hank was a regular on the Braun show. He and Bob generated some goofy humor between them; the two carried on like school buddies. When Hank was on the show, he told Bob about my book. Bob immediately asked one of his staff to schedule me to come on.

I greeted Hank's news with my customary timidity. "But I've never been on television," I wailed. Hank waved his hand in a nothing-to-worry-about gesture. "You'll have a great time with Bob," he said.

I looked at the calendar. The scheduled date was two weeks away—time for me to rehearse. As a reporter, I was certain the first question would be, "What is homeopathy?" I wrote down the answer and then committed it to memory. *Homeopathy is a system of medicine that uses tiny doses of natural substances to strengthen the immune system.* I walked around the house intoning my mantra, *Homeopathy is a system of medicine . . . .*

The scheduled date finally arrived. Seated at my dressing table, my hands were ice cold and shaking. To apply lipstick, I had to steady my right hand with my left. I looked at my reflection in the bathroom mirror. *Homeopathy is a system of medicine . . . .*

When I arrived at the studio, a perky young woman named Jill took me to the Green Room where guests waited to appear on the show. Why was I so nervous? The couple next to me were chatting and laughing while they watched the show on the monitor. Then Jill returned and beckoned to the couple, who quickly got to their feet and followed her.

It's like the executioner calling for the condemned prisoner, I thought grimly. *Please don't make me next.* But they did.

On stage, I waited in the darkened area of the wings. Then, following a hand signal from the director, I walked on stage. The bright lights dazzled. I blinked, suddenly aware of the audience stretched row after row in the dimly-lit theatre.

Bob stood up and grasped my hands with his. "You all know Dr. Henry Heimlich," Bob said to the audience. "Here is Dr. Heimlich's wife, who has written an important medical book. It's about ho-me-opathy," he said, pronouncing the name carefully. "Jane, what exactly is "homeopathy?" I smiled.

Homeopathy is a system of medicine . . . My lips were moving but no words came out. My tongue was so dry it stuck to the roof of my mouth. I tried again but it sounded as if I were drunk. *Homeopashe ish a shistom of mesh* . . . Bob saw what had happened and smoothly carried on a one-person conversation.

In the ensuing months, whenever someone said to me, "I saw you on *The Bob Braun Show,*" I felt as if the person had witnessed me doing something unspeakable such as sitting on the toilet in public and I changed the subject as fast as I could.

Luckily, the fortunes of *Homeopathic Medicine at Home* did not depend upon my performing abilities. Instead, the strength of my book, from a sales point of view, was that homeopathy is practiced all over the world and consequently could be marketed abroad. Over the years, I've received copies of *Homoeopathie thuis* (Dutch),

Homöopathische Hausapotheke (German), as well as editions sold in Great Britain, India, and Israel. This book, which caused me such pain in its gestation, has paid modest but dependable royalties twice a year since 1980.

During those solitary years of working on *Homeopathic Medicine at Home*, I daydreamed about a visit with Janice. She was my wise therapist, my spiritual guide. I had always visualized her as a large lady in a flowing gown. Perhaps it was the puns, corny but loveable.

My chance to meet Janice came shortly after my book was published when Hank and I were in Los Angeles for a medical meeting. I called Jeremy and we made a date to tour his office and meet the staff. In and out of offices we went until we came to the last one. "And here is your editor, Janice Gallagher." I stared. I could not believe it.

She's only a slip of a girl, I thought to myself, using an expression that came out of nowhere. It was this skinny little teenager in blue jeans, legs curled under her in an arm chair, who had sustained me all those years.

I was about to ask Janice if she were free for lunch with us, but she was deep in conversation with another young woman. "You'll have to excuse us," she said. "We have a slight problem with this manuscript."

I smiled. I knew all about problems like these.

CHAPTER 20

Coming
full circle

Daughter Elisabeth, Henry, and son Philip with Jane at a book signing.

The leading lady

of my generation was

the housewife. There

were other women,

though, and other work.

In time, all of them

could dance.

As a writer, I crave solitude. Silence is as restorative as a sip of cold water on a hot day. The fact that my husband and children were away on a trip meant that I had close to a month to work uninterrupted on my new manuscript. There was a deep satisfaction in my slow but steady progress. When I wasn't absorbed by the computer screen, I gazed through the picture window at towering oak trees. There was a plucky little red leaf that, day after day, hung on to its branch until finally the wind whipped it away. I felt like that leaf—tenacious, determined.

At the end of a day of writing, I prepared simple vegetarian meals for myself that were admittedly not family favorites. I leafed through *The New York Times*, eating alone at an unhurried speed and listening to classical music on the radio.

There was a certain purity to my days. Newly written pages piled up. To keep from being distracted, I resisted calling friends. Writing itself required a nun-like sequestering. But in this solitude I discovered who I *really* was.

Letting go of one passion led me to another that was even more consuming.

The Good Wife popped up now and then. I knew I was in trouble when I started comparing myself to her impossibly perfect image. Where did she come from? In my case, the movies of the 1940s and '50s. She was Myrna Loy, dubbed "the perfect wife," in a slim hostess gown looking as if she had just emerged from a beauty salon but had actually prepared a *cordon bleu* dish—perhaps a savory *bourguignonne*—for the guests. She created exquisite flower arrangements. The Good Wife excelled in all the pursuits that beautified the home and pleased husband and children.

The Good Wife was also my mother. Every morning, she squeezed fresh orange juice for my father, a late sleeper. She waited until his eyelids fluttered open to ensure that the foaming juice would be absolutely fresh.

Mother could have been a fine writer. One of her achievements was her book. After my father retired, Mother planned to continue writing, but she found it impossible do so with my father criticizing everything she wrote or, worse, telling her what she should write about. After struggling with one of his untenable book ideas, "How celebrities toast their guests," Mother gave up writing and devoted her time to keeping a record of her husband's investments.

Women of my generation were brought up to perform and please, like geishas. My twin daughters would hoot at this idealized American wife, but my contemporaries and I took it seriously. When my husband watched televison, he sat in a comfortable recliner we called "Daddy's chair." I perched on a hassock and never considered buying myself a Mommy chair.

What gave me the courage to defy the Good Wife ideal was my desire to write, to bring all this little-known information about alternative medicine to a deserving public. For some time, though, regrets reappeared, plunging me into feelings of guilt. I was folding sweaters in daughter Elisabeth's closet when I saw the photo album that she and her twin sister had kept through the years. Captioning the photos, Elisabeth had written in her little-girl script: *Elisabeth and Janet with Daddy in Alaska, 1976, Elisabeth and Janet with Daddy in Australia. Elisabeth and Janet with Daddy in New Zealand. Elisabeth with Daddy in Antarctica.*

Where was I, the mother? Flipping through the remaining pages, I could see I wasn't in any of these photos. Not one. While my husband and twin daughters were off on trips, I was home in Cincinnati writing a book about alternative medicine.

There was a photo of my husband taken in front of Ayers Rock. Still handsome in his early 50s—those beetling black eyebrows, the cleft in his cheek, the dimpled smile—were all familiar. How could I have let this husband of mine go off without me? A good wife would have dropped everything to be with her husband and her family. Sick with the awareness of what I had missed and could never experience again, my eyes filled with tears.

When Hank returned, I asked him whether he felt I had deserted him by not going on the trip. He looked surprised. "You had a job to do," he said.

Facing my shortcomings as a mother was the most painful aspect of letting go of the stereotype of perfection. Having been raised before Dr. Spock introduced a more relaxed approach to child-rearing, I was always in a rush, like the white rabbit in Alice in Wonderland. Wanting to be a good mother but having no role models, I often forgot about having fun with my children. When our son, Peter, was 9, he once said to me, "I like you when you're not being a mother."

Ironically, I had written an article for *Parents* magazine about treating your twins as individuals. Janet, one of our twins once said to me, "Why do you always call us 'girls' instead of by our right names?" It was painful to realize I had ignored my own advice.

In the midst of my soul-searching, something occurred that I could never have anticipated. Writing my books on alternative medicine was more than a reporting job; it was my passion. I could now understand my father's single-minded devotion to ballroom dancing.

But after giving so much time and energy to alternative medicine, I had tired of writing about it. It had been more fun being a single voice in the wilderness, and after close to twenty-five years in the field, I wanted to move on. But where did I want to go next? The path wasn't clear.

My editor at HarperCollins and my literary agent pointed out that the market for alternative medicine was expanding. "It's time for a new edition," my editor said. My agent bubbled with ideas to sell the revised edition.

Gamely, I tried to muster enthusiasm for the task. I had worked hard to establish my reputation in the field, and I wanted to hang on to the mantle of health guru. It was easy to convince myself that revising the book was mainly updating data, but when I took a closer look I could see that the revisions would be enormous. Entire chapters dealing with new subjects would have to be written.

Unable to turn down either publisher or agent, my body cleverly found a way to resolve the impasse. I developed a tremor in my right hand.

It's just stress, I thought.

But as the tremor became more pronounced, I had difficulty taking notes. Finally, at my husband's urging, I made an appointment with a well respected neurologist and received the dreaded diagnosis: Parkinson's.

At first I was angry and indignant. I searched for those "experts" who disagreed with the diagnosis. A brain specialist in Los Angeles, after running a series of tests, said, "I will stake my reputation that you do *not* have Parkinson's." My neurologist did not agree with the Los Angeles specialist.

Finally, I stopped denying my condition and in the process realized I had much to be grateful for. "Unlike younger people who have the disease," the neurologist said, "you have the type of Parkinson's where symptoms are controlled by two well-tested drugs."

I, who had railed against medical drugs all these years, now had to admit that certain drugs could be lifesavers.

Ten years have passed since the diagnosis. Now my right hand shows no signs of a tremor unless I'm stressed. In fact, the tremor is like the canary in the coal mine that keels over when the oxygen gets thin. When I am under stress, my right hand flaps like a fish. It's a warning to stay calm.

Letting go of alternative health led me to write this book. It started out as a "tell all"—how unloving and insensitive I thought my father was. Knowing so little about his family and background, it was no wonder I never understood him. We never celebrated holidays with any of his family members and yet I detected strong family ties. It was my good luck to find Uncle Ira, my father's "kid brother," living in Florida and vigorously nearing 100. Talking to him, I began to understand what it was like to grow up in a tough slum neighborhood and contend with a sharp-tongued mother who told her sons they'd never amount to anything.

In one of my first conversations with Ira, he ended our talk by saying, "I love you." I was startled. My father would never have said that he loved me. And yet it was his voice. I felt affectionate toward Ira but also sad.

As a teenager, my father was painfully shy and stammered badly. But when he discovered that ballroom dancing gave him poise and confidence, he was on his way to success. In the 1960s, though, the popularity of rock 'n' roll and freestyle dancing made ballroom dancing seem fuddy-duddy. With declining business, some branch managers resorted to high pressure sales methods which, in Minneapolis, came to the attention of the district attorney.

Anxious to shrug off the problems of a floundering business, in 1964 when my father was 69, he sold the dance studio chain to a group of investors in Boca Raton, Florida. My parents then retired to Honolulu, half a world away. The island of Oahu has perfect weather, my father explained, and an active cultural life. My parents rapidly became the stellar hosts of the island. Society columnists described their dancing parties, their art collection, and quoted my father's deadpan humor.

Phyllis and I made the long journey to see our parents two or three times a year, always together. We needed each other. As we crossed the ocean, time fell away and we became schoolgirls again, allied once more against the adults. The truth was that our parents, after all this time, still made us nervous. The slightest thing might provoke Daddy to a sardonic reply. One never knew what he might say. Once, in the middle of a pleasant conversation, he said, "You have the most poorly behaved children I've ever seen." I was stunned. Then Mother would attempt to mitigate the falling temperatures around us.

The trips to Honolulu reminded me of our early years, when we relied on each other. I didn't feel whole without Phyllis and she felt the same about me. We saw ourselves as two imps pitted against the world of grownups, jabbering away in our twin language or staying up half the night talking or playing let's pretend.

We dressed alike, we looked alike, we sounded alike. We shared a low opinion of grownups. Adults greeting us bent down and asked the same boring question over and over. "How do I tell you apart?" We generally mumbled, "I don't know." One time, Phyllis, who loved raw onions and already showed a sassy streak, gave a different answer. "Smell us," she said, and exhaled in the lady's face.

Prior to adolescence I don't recall that we competed with one another although I've read that twins are more competitive than single children. As preteens, instead of competing, we joined forces to outwit our parents and teachers. Our best weapon was our twin language. It wasn't a real language. We simply mumbled, moving our lips as little as possible, like a ventriloquist. Years later, when we met Edgar Bergen, a well known TV ventriloquist, and saw him perform with his dummy, Charlie McCarthy, we instantly recognized the roots of our twin language.

My father became angry when Phyllis and I launched into our twin language. Being raised as he was, he had undoubtedly worked hard to learn to speak properly. One day, after hearing us mumble and giggle, he yelled at Mother, "Those girls need elocution lessons!" and stalked out of our room. We rolled over the floor unable to stop giggling. Phyllis pointed a finger at me and assumed a deep voice. "Oo nee elocushon leshon!" We were both curious about this mysterious "elocution," but my father never made good his threat.

Our classmates in fifth grade never seemed to tire of our twin pranks. These pranks were based on the fact that most people couldn't tell us apart. First thing in the morning, we conferred in the closet, bare feet on the cold wood floor, and discussed our choices.

Jane: "What about the navy blue jumper?"

Phyllis: "We wore that last week."

We quickly decided on our tartan plaid skirts with the gold safety pins and white blouses with Peter Pan collars.

One of the high points of our twin act was the day we switched classes. We were in fifth grade. I agreed to take Phyllis's test on French verbs; Phyllis, who had a flair for drawing, took my place in art class. I had been struggling for weeks to draw a cleaning woman standing with her mop. Using different shades of blue, I tried to express her fatigue, her hopelessness, but I had rubbed the paper thin and it was difficult to recognize the figure.

In preparation for the French test, I barricaded myself behind a wall of books lest the teacher suspect my identity. Here and there a giggle erupted in the classroom that brought a warning, "Quiet, please," from the teacher.

The next day, we resumed our rightful places in class. Phyllis was gratified to receive an A on the French test. I walked down the hall to art class and with beating heart looked for my cleaning lady drawing. I caught my breath. She was beautiful. The defeated slouch of her shoulders, her sad expression conveyed exactly what I had been unable to express.

Day after day we attracted attention as the class comedians. Except one morning when Phyllis had a cold. Mother shook her head at me.

"No, dear, there's no reason for you to stay home just because your sister isn't feeling well." Phyllis and I exchanged mournful looks. When we were both home sick, our favorite pastime was drinking glasses of freshly squeezed orange juice and listening to radio soaps like Backstage Wife and Our Gal Sunday. It wouldn't be any fun for just one of us without the other. With heavy heart I went off to school and quietly took my place at the desk that was next to Phyllis's empty desk.

"Which one are you?" Billy asked me.

I mumbled a dispirited answer.

"Where's Phyllis?"

She's home sick," I said.

Differences evolved only as we grew older. I found my niche in writing, enjoying the pleasure of words as well as the ego boost of a byline. Phyllis became the class clown as well as the bad girl; at boarding school she narrowly escaped being expelled for smoking.

The stage was set for a confrontation when during that memorable summer in Beverly Hills when we were teenagers, and I had a special boyfriend named Steve. Maybe everything would have stayed the same if Phyllis hadn't answered the door bell. If Phyllis hadn't worn a bright red sweater. If she hadn't squirted Tabu cologne behind her ears.

Phyllis was sitting at the dressing table already wearing her red sweater. Phyllis and I usually decided together what we were going to wear, but today she hadn't waited for me. I looked at the clock on the dressing table. *Eleven thirty!* Steve was calling for me at noon and I still had rollers in my hair.

"Are you going on a real date?" Phyllis asked me, then went back to looking in the mirror and making pouty Ava Gardner lips.

"I guess so," I said, pulling off the rollers, which got so tangled they brought tears to my eyes.

Brushing my hair, I remembered the night I met Steve at one of Groucho's informal family parties at the beginning of the summer. Sitting on the couch, watching the grownups and feeling a little shy, I looked up. "I haven't met you," he said. "I'm Steve Pascal."

He had a nice crooked smile, a lock of sun-bleached hair that kept falling in his eyes. He wore a crisp, short-sleeved, checked shirt that accentuated his tan. When he sat down next to me and crossed his legs, I saw that his shoes were polished like my father's.

The night we met I wore my favorite sweater, a knit, the color of yellow daffodils.

It was a happy sweater. A zipper zigzagging down one side made my small breasts look nice and rounded.

Phyllis was sitting in an armchair leafing through *The Hollywood Reporter*. I knew she was peeved because Steve was the only boy at the party and he was paying attention to me.

"What time is Daddy picking us up?" she said crossly.

At Groucho's next party, Steve and I sat on the couch holding hands. Groucho wasted no time in unleashing his unique brand of humor. "Rumors have reached me that nuptials are in the offing, and the young man in question has not even spoken to me." I blushed furiously. "I am of course investigating the young man's character." On and on he played with the leitmotiv of romance while my face burned and I giggled happily.

"Thanks for your thoughts, Grouch," Steve said, pulling me to my feet. "Let's get something to eat."

In the dining room, there was a platter of pastrami, roast beef, and dill pickles, largely untouched. No one ate much at Groucho's—they were too busy talking. At that moment Phyllis walked into the dining room. "What do you recommend?" she asked Steve. "Pastrami? I've never tasted it." She picked up a slice of the spicy meat and dangled it close to his lips. She giggled. "Try it."

Toward the end of the party, Steve took my hand and led me to his father's car parked in the driveway. We slid into the back seat. He put his arms around me and held me tightly. His lips felt warm and he was breathing hard. Necking in full view of the grownups made me uncomfortable; they could see us through the side window. I wanted Steve's father to think favorably of me.

"I think we ought to go back," I said. Instead, Steve tipped my head back.

"Open your mouth," he whispered, his tongue, like a little garter snake, exploring my tongue. In some perverse way, I bridled at being told what to do and clamped my teeth shut.

"What time do you think you'll be back?" Phyllis asked, looking in the mirror and putting on a deep red lipstick. This was the day when Steve was allowed to drive his father's car. Why was I feeling uneasy? Early that morning I had heard Phyllis talking on the phone. She gave her throaty laugh, and then she suddenly stopped talking when I came into the room.

I was pulling a sweater over my head when the doorbell rang. The sweater was the color of American beauty roses and I wore a matching lipstick. After that day, I thought of the color as the color of the poisoned apple that the wicked stepmother gave to Snow White.

Phyllis licked her forefinger and smoothed an eyebrow. "I'll go," she called. I could hear her footsteps as she ran to the door, the sound of the door being opened. Phyllis must have said something funny. I heard Steve laugh. They both emerged from the hallway, their faces flushed, as if they shared a secret joke.

A few minutes later Steve and I were on our way to Santa Monica. Steve didn't talk much. I felt as if I were chattering, like my mother does. We had planned to walk along the beach but Steve made no move. We sat in the car watching the waves crash. I felt tongue-tied. What was wrong? Steve looked at his watch. "I've got a load of homework," he said, starting the car. "I better get to it."

After our Sunday date, Steve didn't call for a few days and then the phone rang and I heard his voice. But he didn't ask for me. "May I speak to Phyllis?" he said. I felt as if I couldn't breathe. I held the receiver in my hand until she was on the phone giving that low-pitched laugh. I couldn't believe this was happening. I lay down on my bed and put my hand on my thumping heart. Then I knew why they talked about being broken-hearted. My heart felt broken. She is Steve's girl, I said to myself. Steve's girl.

A few nights later, the four of us, my parents, Phyllis and I, sat at a table in the restaurant of the Beverly Hills Hotel. The room was decorated with potted palms and wicker furniture. "Steve is picking me up," Phyllis said, keeping her eyes on her plate. My parents looked at one another.

"When did this happen?" my father said.

"Oh, I don't know," she said. "I don't keep track of things."

"How is your steak, dear?" Mother asked Daddy. "Is it too rare?" My father carefully cut into the meat and peered into the cavity. Mother leaned over Daddy's plate.

"Arthur, that's much too rare. Why don't you call the waiter."

I looked up. Steve in a white-ribbed sweater, wearing a tense smile, walked toward our table. My heart lurched. He looked even more handsome than I remembered. Phyllis jumped up to meet him. Mother said, "Dear, you haven't finished your dinner," but Phyllis had already caught up with Steve.

After Phyllis and Steve left, I toyed with my food. Mother looked at me with large sorrowful eyes. I didn't want her sympathy—I wanted Steve. I wonder where they're going, whether he puts his arm around her shoulders. I put down my fork. Nothing eases the pain.

If the seducer had been a classmate, or even a friend, the event would not have been so traumatic. But when the betrayal was perpetrated by my own twin sister, I was deeply hurt. We had built a relationship founded on trust and Phyllis had betrayed this trust. The incident robbed me of confidence.

I never discussed the Steve episode with Phyllis; it remained a frozen lump in my throat. As young married adults, Phyllis and I, and our respective husbands and children, lived within a two-hour drive from one another. Nevertheless, we rarely made the effort to see one another. The cousins grew up scarcely knowing one another.

Happily, as the years went by, this situation changed. Time itself, as it often does, effected a reconciliation. It was a reconciliation of a breach that had never been properly acknowledged. But we were not a confrontational family; Mother gave us early lessons in the art of evasion. She had flung herself out of her kitchen window in an attempt on her own life, then spoke of it as a household accident.

I became very fond of Phyllis's four daughters; we joked about the same things as if we had the same humor locked in our bones. And now, my secret sorrow safely locked away with my younger self, I was glad my sister would be with me, a bulwark against our formidable father.

It was years before I made the trip to Hawaii by myself. When I did, the visits assumed a pattern: I took a cab from the airport to the Kaimana Hotel adjacent to their Diamond Head penthouse. Mother awaited in the hotel lobby laden with bars of her favorite soap, four silk hangers, several white telephone pads, and sharpened pencils.

After surveying my ocean view room, which she had reserved and would pay for, she asked, "Can you be ready at 7? I've invited the Simpsons to join us for dinner. You like them, don't you?"

"Oh yes," I assure her, feeling something constrict in my chest. I would rather be alone with my parents or, rather, wish they wanted to be alone with me. Besides with the five-hour time change, seven o'clock will be midnight for me and I don't relish making conversation. But I merely kiss my mother goodbye and promise to be on time.

On the dot of seven, I ring their doorbell at the Sans Souci Apartments. I'm wearing my best outfit, an aqua silk pants suit with matching blouse. Mother answers the door, then carols, "Arthur, Jane is here." She smiles at me.

"You don't look tired at all. Your father has been waiting for you." He is sitting in his favorite armchair, a newspaper on his lap. I lean down to kiss him. "Arthur, doesn't Jane look nice?" my mother asks. He takes off his glasses.

"Stand over there," he says. I pirouette obediently. He nods approvingly. "Where did you get that? It's very becoming."

The next evening, wearing my second-best outfit, I get a different reaction from my father. His lap is covered with bank statements. He looks cranky.

"Another new outfit? Why do you need so many clothes?"

And yet, I had never seen my father so happy. He credited his good health to swimming twice a day in the clean sparkling water of Waikiki, which gently lapped on the fine white sand.

His endurance for a man in his early 90s was remarkable. One time Phyllis and I watched him swim to a distant reef and then disappear from sight. We looked at each other fearfully, then rushed to the lifeguard, who quickly dived into the surf to rescue Mr. Murray. My father, who was circling the reef with his unorthodox crawl, did not appreciate our efforts.

"I swim this far every day," he said crossly. "You ruined my swim."

The health measures cited regularly by my father were the Jewish dietary laws in the Old Testament. "Never eat shellfish," he said. "Jacques Cousteau describes shell fish as the scavengers of the deep."

Another Jewish dietary law that he frequently referred to prohibited mixing dairy and meat. This law did not deter my father from eating lamb chops followed by coffee ice cream, his favorite dessert. He invariably burped after scooping the last spoonful of ice cream. "See, I told you. You shouldn't mix dairy and meat."

Until his 90th birthday, my father was on the phone most of the time. At dinner that night, he explained that he had become a private investment counselor. "I handle portfolios of family members and friends. All gratis," he added. "It keeps my mind sharp."

The next day, rifling through papers on his lap, he said, "I made $10,000 for you this morning." He looked faintly amused.

"Thank you," I said lamely.

It occurred to me if I showed an interest in the stock market we'd have something to talk about.

"Have you ever lost money on any one's investment?" I asked.

"Once. I made the mistake of following a tip from a company president. I reimbursed this couple for every cent they had lost."

Another day I was left alone with my father while Mother was at the beauty shop.

Gazing at Utrillo's Street Scene, I asked him how he had acquired his famed collection of French Impressionists.

"Did someone advise you?"

"I bought what I liked," he said. "One late afternoon in the fall of 1959, I saw this Utrillo in the window of the Park Benet gallery on Madison Avenue. French

Impressionists weren't so high-priced then. This painting was listed at 3,250 pounds. I bought it on the spot."

One by one, as Pissarro followed Boudin followed Cassatt followed Corot, my father described, without a pause, the circumstance of the sale, as fondly as couples describe how they met. When my mother returned, we were still circling the living room. My father remained remarkably healthy until a few months before his 96th birthday when he developed a cough and a wheeze. It was pneumonia. His doctor prescribed antibiotics, which cleared up his symptoms but only temporarily.

"We better put you in the hospital," his doctor said.

Mother and I sat on uncomfortable straight chairs in the waiting room bathed in misery. "He hates air conditioning," Mother said. "If he were home . . . ."

But we felt helpless to insist that the soft breezes from the lanai would be more therapeutic than the icy waves of air conditioning that chilled him in his hospital room.

Eventually he was discharged and sat, eyes closed, covered with a cashmere blanket, in the living room. Mother was in and out of the kitchen, offering orange juice.

"Just take a sip, dear."

I looked around the room, once an elegant white interior. Now there were urine stains on the rug, and the seats of the Chippendale chairs were stained. Their world had shrunk from parties and island glamour to the paraphernalia of pill bottles and urinals.

My father opened his eyes. I strained to hear.

"We were so poor we used newspaper for toilet paper," he said. And then he was gone. His thoughts were not about the elegant young man who made dance history or the wealth this penniless young man had acquired. He had spent his life getting as far away as he could from the impoverished East Side tenement of his youth. And yet—more than half a century later and half a world away—it was as if he had never left at all.

CHAPTER 21

The last dance

Jane and Henry, off on a hike.

What's the secret to happiness as one grows older? Keeping busy. And knowing the difference between mere busy-ness and the art of keeping busy.

When I was 4 or 5, I felt sure I knew what it was like to be an old lady. Old ladies wore pink corsets that fit like harnesses. Our nurse, Helen, had a corset that pinched her on the sides so she only wore it on her day off. When she removed her corset at the end of the day, she sighed and said, "That feels good." Helen's corset rested on a table as if it had a life of its own.

Old ladies painted red circles on their cheeks like clowns. Phyllis and I giggled and called them "Rouge Ray." Besides making up their cheeks, old ladies had permanent waves using a contraption I saw in a beauty shop that had rollers that clamped on metal rods and hung from the ceiling like Medusa's snakes.

Old ladies smelled good. Nana, my grandmother, wore Guerlain's L'Heure Bleue. She kept tiny satin sachets tucked in her stocking drawer. Though Nana was attractively perfumed, she had other habits that were not so pleasing. She told us that she took a tablespoon of Phillips' Milk of Magnesia every night. It made me slightly sick just thinking of it. Sometimes I wasn't so sure I wanted to be a grownup.

When old ladies went out to restaurants with their spouses neither of them talked. I remember watching an old couple in the vast circular dining room of the Coronado Hotel in California. No one said a word throughout the entire meal. I wondered: *Is this what it's like being married?*

A sweet-tempered disposition is a sure balm on the various conditions of aging.

Old people liked to tell scary stories. While my dentist in New Rochelle was poking around in my mouth, he told my mother about the baby nurse who turned on the gas and put the baby in the oven. The gas, he said, quieted the baby. Did Dr. Chapin think I couldn't hear? I thought of that story every night at bedtime.

I liked my grandfather best of all the old people in our family. Grampe wrote me letters signed with his looping signature, *Your true friend and pal, Grampe*. He smelled of pipe tobacco and whiskey. I loved Grampe, but Nana and my father said bad things about him behind his back.

"He's drinking again," Nana would say, mouthing the words without any sound coming out. I wanted to tell them not to be so mean, but I didn't dare.

One cold gray October afternoon Grampe showed us how to roast potatoes—he called them "mickies"—in a pile of rocks. "You get a nice fire going, then throw your potato in the coals. Let it cook. You can tell when its done by the smell." Grampe speared a potato for Phyllis with a pointed stick, whipped out a handkerchief from his suit pocket and handed a mickey to her. He did the same for me. "Don't burn your fingers, girls." I can still smell those mickies.

I thought, *When I grow old, I want to be like Grampe.*

Now I'm the old lady who goes out to dinner with her husband and sits without talking except for an occasional comment about the food or server. I revel in the silence. We've purposely chosen a restaurant that's quiet and plays no music. I study the faces of other patrons, noticing their food choices. I chew each bite; no need to make conversation. Sometimes Hank and I hold hands, a little self-consciously, as if we were posing for the cover of a retirement magazine. "Isn't that sweet?" I hear a young woman whisper.

What's it like to grow old? Oldsters will not likely hear this question from their children. Younger people know it will never happen to them. But inevitably it does happen. Everyone grows old and with increasing age usually becomes heir to a variety of maladies. Hank and I each have our corresponding disability to deal with. A state-of-the-art hearing aid helps Hank's deafness and allows him to hear most conversations, particularly men's more audible voices. But at bedtime when Hank has unscrewed his hearing aide and deposited it like precious jewelry in its little box, he can't hear me unless I shout or spell each word like a participant in a spelling bee. The mumbled pillow talk I used to enjoy is gone forever.

As for me, I'm afflicted with an arthritic shoulder. Some of the simplest movements, such as taking off a turtleneck shirt, are painful, or even impossible, to manage. So I wait patiently for Hank to finish his phone conversation to help me. It's downright humiliating to sink into my padded chaise lounge and then not be able to get out without assistance. Whatever happened to Jane the health guru who had a potion for every ill? Flaxseed oil for dry skin, apple cider vinegar to settle the stomach. I felt invincible during those younger years.

Many older folks have reached the age of "All Passion Spent." Some of us women welcome such a situation, as I've gathered from listening to conversations at women's groups. I can't recall a woman who complained about her husband not demanding *enough* sex. More often, though, women are pleased with the sense of power that their sexuality imparts, but at the same time they joke about the headache and other subterfuges they employ to get a good night's sleep. So for anyone who yearns for more sleep rather than more sex, the later years may prove restful.

After retirement, when couples spend most of their time together, can be a time of disagreement and friction. Until Hank retired and began spending more time in the kitchen, we rarely quarreled. He didn't intend to take over the cooking that inspired his kitchen visits. No, it was fear of waste that Hank claims that he traces to his childhood during the Great Depression.

This is the conversation that usually takes place:

Hank: *What happened to those strawberries? I left three strawberries in a little plastic container.*

Jane: *Those strawberies? I threw them out. They were all moldy!*

Hank: *There was nothing wrong with those strawberries. That's terrible,* Hank mutters, and shakes his head over the amount of waste that goes on in our kitchen.

I think to myself: *How can a doctor save more lives than any other being on earth and still worry about a few strawberries?*

The disagreement over strawberries is long forgotten in the wake of my husband's usual sweet-tempered disposition. I am in charge of meals in our household, a gender based tradition and clearly not tied to any aptitude for cooking. Nevertheless, I feel that a poorly prepared dinner is my responsibility.

One night's vegetarian special, stuffed peppers, was, to put it mildly, disappointing. The proportions were all wrong: too much sticky rice, not enough tomato sauce or beans.

Does Hank use this lumpy dish to illustrate my shortcomings? No, he ferrets out the one redeeming feature of this dish. He takes a bite, chews thoughtfully, and says, "It's nice and hot."

When I began observing my behavior as an aging woman, I noticed a strong competitive element in this process. Perhaps it's because I have a twin sister. Phyllis puts me to shame. Not only has she kept up her ballroom dancing—she and her partner compete in dance contests. Along with dancing twice a week, she walks daily on a treadmill, and is so crazy about golf she totes her clubs on every vacation.

Family portrait: daughter-in-law Rebecca and grandson Henry, son Philip (in sunglasses), and Jane and Henry. Seated is daughter Janet and granddaughter Maxine Jane McQuarters.

I admire her health routine and, yes, I vow to increase my short walks and try water aerobics even though I hate getting wet. But I would not trade the less athletic experience of writing this memoir for, as we used to say, all the tea in China. Nailing down a memory with words that convey the feeling of the event so that it's always with you is greatly satisfying.

I remember when my world was babies and diapers and I said to myself, *Is this what I went to college for?* Not realizing how short-lived this period of caring for small children would be, I felt a stab of jealousy when Hank got home from what I saw as an exciting time in the outside world. "What's new?" he invariably asked. When I finally found time to do a little writing, even thinking about the poem I wanted to write or contemplating an interview was a gift ready to be unwrapped.

What is the key to happiness? According to many women I talk to or eavesdrop on, it's keeping busy. But there's a big difference between busy-ness and keeping busy. Busy-ness is the search for distraction. Keeping busy in later life is being open to some new small passion that will give your life more fire and meaning.

Shortly after Hank gave up tennis, a friend presented us with a birdhouse. We hung it up. We were mesmerized watching mama and papa wren gathering provisions for their young, flying in and out of what looked like an impossibly small hole. One of these days when another tennis buddy asks Hank the perennial question, "Still playing tennis?" I hope Hank will give a deadpan reply such as "Nope. Too busy watching the birds."

In his retirement years, my father became an investment counselor, handling portfolios at no charge for family and friends. This demanding pursuit would hardly suit the needs of most retirees but for a man who needed more mental stimulation than a crossword puzzle could supply, it was the right choice.

How do I plan to spend my time after I finish this memoir? I tell friends I'm going to play more. I'm going to go to afternoon movies and spend a day at a spa. It may be unrealistic because of my advancing Parkinson's, but I still have a dream of tutoring a child in English or teaching a writing class at a nearby prison.

And I really am serious about studying those bird sounds.

It's a new world with new pleasures and opportunities. It's my last dance. I want to make the most of it.